Awkwardness

Awkwardness

A Theory

ALEXANDRA PLAKIAS

OXFORD
UNIVERSITY PRESS

Oxford University Press is a department of the University of Oxford. It furthers
the University's objective of excellence in research, scholarship, and education
by publishing worldwide. Oxford is a registered trade mark of Oxford University
Press in the UK and certain other countries.

Published in the United States of America by Oxford University Press
198 Madison Avenue, New York, NY 10016, United States of America.

© Oxford University Press 2024

All rights reserved. No part of this publication may be reproduced, stored in
a retrieval system, or transmitted, in any form or by any means, without the
prior permission in writing of Oxford University Press, or as expressly permitted
by law, by license, or under terms agreed with the appropriate reproduction
rights organization. Inquiries concerning reproduction outside the scope of the
above should be sent to the Rights Department, Oxford University Press, at the
address above.

You must not circulate this work in any other form
and you must impose this same condition on any acquirer.

Library of Congress Cataloging-in-Publication Data
Names: Plakias, Alexandra, author.
Title: Awkwardness : a theory / by Alexandra Plakias.
Description: New York, NY : Oxford Uiversity Press, [2024] |
Includes bibliographical references and index. |
Contents: Introduction—This is Awkward—Feeling Awkward—
Awkward, Socially—Morally Awkward Problems—Awkward Silence—
The Importance of Being Awkward.
Identifiers: LCCN 2023043048 | ISBN 9780197683606 (hardback) |
ISBN 9780197683637 (ebook) | ISBN 9780197683613 (epub)
Subjects: LCSH: Clumsiness—Social aspects. | Faux pas. | Social interaction.
Classification: LCC BJ1838.P53 2024 | DDC 395—dc23/eng/20231107
LC record available at https://lccn.loc.gov/2023043048

DOI: 10.1093/oso/9780197683606.001.0001

Printed by Integrated Books International, United States of America

The manufacturer's authorised representative in the EU for product safety is
Oxford University Press España S.A. of el Parque Empresarial San Fernando
de Henares, Avenida de Castilla, 2 - 28830 Madrid (www.oup.es/en)

Contents

Acknowledgments   vii

   Introduction   1

1. This Is Awkward   7
2. Feeling Awkward   38
3. Awkward, Socially   64
4. Morally Awkward Problems   91
5. Awkward Silence   119
6. The Importance of Being Awkward   148

Bibliography   169
Index   183

Acknowledgments

Being acknowledged for your contribution to a book about awkwardness is a dubious honor, so let me clarify that none of the individuals named here inspired any of the content of the book—the examples are largely fictional, and where they're not, the experiences involved are either hypothetical or my own, unless specified otherwise.

But the book benefited from conversations with many people, on a wide-ranging set of topics. Thanks to every single person who expressed enthusiasm for a book about awkwardness, starting with Peter Ohlin at Oxford University Press.

Thanks to Dan Kelly and an anonymous reviewer for feedback on the proposal and an earlier draft of the book, and to John Lawless for reading chapters and providing suggestions. Audiences at the Moral Psychology Research Group provided helpful feedback on the overall argument presented here, and conversations with Aaron Meskin and two of his wonderful University of Georgia graduate students, Hannah Raskoski and Marissa "Rissa" Willis, helped inform my thinking about cringe (and convinced me that it was a term worth discussing).

I am fortunate to be part of a wonderful, warm, completely non-awkward department. No thanks to them for the examples in this book, which I had to come up with on my own. But many thanks to Justin Clark, Katheryn Doran, Todd Franklin, Marianne Janack, Russell Marcus, and Alessandro Moscarítolo Palacio for their encouragement and enthusiasm throughout the project. Justin Clark pointed me toward helpful sources on the psychology of attunement and loneliness and the ancient Greek translation of "awkward." The

Levitt Public Affairs Center at Hamilton College funded preliminary research for the book, which I conducted alongside my outstanding student Honor Allen; Honor's perspective saved me from writing a much cringier book.

I started working on this book a few months into the COVID-19 pandemic, when leaving the house was a luxury, child care was nonexistent, and the future was uncertain. There's something strange about writing a book about awkwardness when you're not interacting with anyone. I was fortunate to have a wonderful support network in the form of a text-thread with my fellow professor-parents. Thank you to Cat, Celeste, Erica, Kate, and Jaime; thanks also to Kendahl for keeping me focused on reality.

I am also lucky enough to have the friendship of the inimitable and formidable Nina Strohminger, who consistently challenges and inspires me, and makes me laugh very hard.

My sister Anastasia Plakias has seen me through some of my most awkward moments. She and my brother-in-law Neil Thompson have been a constant source of support, encouragement, and excellent food. I am constantly inspired by my parents and their fearlessness, curiosity, and sense of adventure. Thank you for making me brave.

There were many times during the writing of this book when I doubted that it would come to fruition. My husband, Douglas Edwards, never did. Thank you for believing in me, for the endless conversations about awkwardness, and for not making me watch awkward British comedy with you. And to our kids, Theo and Lola: you will experience a lot of awkwardness. It's okay. We all do.

To Douglas

Introduction

We live in awkward times. We always have: awkwardness is an inevitable, though perhaps not entirely welcome, part of social change. Awkwardness is the cost and consequence of our social nature; it reveals the extent to which being in sync with our social surroundings matters to us. And it emerges when we have to adjust our behaviors or attitudes to changing social circumstances. Sometimes these adjustments are effortless. Sometimes they're awkward. We're told we live in a "golden age of awkwardness," but adjustments in social norms and roles have always resulted in awkward moments. A *Life* magazine contributor from 1927 bemoans, "These are awkward times, and I sympathize with the teashop waitress who approached a customer from behind and said brightly, 'anything more sir, I mean madam; I beg your pardon sir.'"

Awkwardness is essentially social: it emerges when the scripts we rely on to guide our social interactions fail us, either because they don't exist or we're unable to access or implement them. As a result, we feel awkward: uncertain, uncomfortable, self-conscious. In this respect, awkwardness is a direct consequence of our social nature. Our skill at social navigation is mirrored by our aversion to getting lost.

Appreciating the significance of awkwardness means appreciating the significance of apparently mundane social encounters more generally. Throughout the book, I'll argue that we tend to underestimate the motivational force of our desires to avoid experiencing awkward feelings and to avoid being labeled as awkward. Awkwardness draws our attention to gaps in our social norms and conventions, highlighting areas of our social life that often go unnoticed. It's a kind of normative negative space. So, while awkwardness often functions to silence and suppress, it can also be a tool for moral and social progress.

Recent years have seen a resurgence of interest in the negative emotions: anger, anxiety, disgust, envy. A persuasive case has been made for what Protasi (2021) calls "the wisdom of negative emotion." And while it would be natural to try to apply this narrative here, true to form, awkwardness isn't a neat fit. That's partly because it's not an emotion (or so I'll argue in chapter 2), but also because it's not clear how much wisdom it has to offer us. Instead, it's a sort of warning signal, or diagnostic tool.

Awkwardness is surprisingly underexamined in the scholarly literature. In his book on humiliation, William Miller remarks of the titular emotion that while it "figures in the life of almost all scholars," it "has itself had virtually no scholarly life" (1993: 132). The same could well be said of awkwardness.[1] There's a striking discrepancy between awkwardness's prominence in our culture and its absence from the academic literature.

One reason for this, as we'll see in chapter 2, is that awkwardness is often confused with or assimilated to its close relatives, anxiety and embarrassment. But this is a mistake: awkwardness is importantly different from either of these other emotions. While anxiety, shame, and embarrassment are similarly self-conscious, awkwardness gets at our experience of being in the world in a way these other feelings don't. It's about ourselves, but also about how those selves are seen by others.

This points to a second possible reason for awkwardness's academic neglect: it represents a kind of visceral and emotional

---

[1] The main exceptions are Clegg 2012a, 2012b, and Kotsko 2010, two of the few academic authors to tackle awkwardness directly and in depth. Kotsko's book is an essay on awkwardness, but focuses mainly on how it manifests in popular culture. Dahl 2018 is an overview of the psychology of awkwardness and embarrassment written for a general audience; Tashiro 2017 offers a blend of psychology and self-help; Rhodes 2016 is a memoir/self-help book.

discomfort that we, as intellectuals, think we ought to transcend; its self-conscious concern with social niceties seems rather trivial when compared to issues of social and global justice, or the nature of truth and knowledge. Philosophers tend to focus on the big dilemmas, the virtues, the opportunities for moral greatness—or villainy. It's only more recently that we've started to appreciate the significance of the smaller moments of civility—or offense. Awkwardness sits uneasily alongside these as a way of evaluating our success in the social world. It's a form of social dysfunction, dysfluency, and dysregulation; it's discomfiting.

If philosophers have overlooked the topic, perhaps it's also because awkwardness, and the idea of social discomfort with which it's associated, tends to be associated with a concern for social conformity and smoothness that seems, frankly, beneath our lofty moral and intellectual goals. (This may explain why embarrassment itself is relatively neglected compared to emotions like guilt, shame, and anxiety.) And one of the points I'll make in this book is that awkwardness does work against our ideals: it inhibits moral critique and conversation, and it prevents us from sharing information that would help us revise and improve social and moral norms. And it does so in an unflattering way, by showing how much we care about conforming to social expectations.

Awkwardness highlights the conflict between our moral motivations and our desire for social approval and conformity. Part of what makes awkwardness aversive is that we experience it as a lack of social attunement, which is also what gives it the power to influence and silence us: we want to belong, and we don't want to mark ourselves out. This need for belonging isn't something we tend to celebrate. Our moral heroes are those who dare to stick out and defy convention; this makes us suspicious of the desire to fit in.

But defying convention comes at a cost, which not everyone can afford. As we'll see, working through awkwardness sometimes requires us to "own it"—to acknowledge the uncertainty, or ignorance, involved. That takes a certain level of confidence, and it costs us social currency: admitting that a situation is awkward involves a loss of face, and we don't all have face to spare. This is one way awkwardness can be problematic, and can exacerbate existing inequities. When we deem people "awkward," we consign them to a social status that gives them less access to the social goods (knowledge, confidence, social esteem) needed to navigate potentially awkward situations.

So while I think awkwardness has been unfairly neglected, this is not a redemption story. If anything, it's the opposite: I'm going to try to make the case that awkwardness is worse than we think. It's not a social triviality, some kind of minor, cosmetic imperfection on our social facades. Instead, it reveals a way in which we ostracize and punish those who fail to fit into existing social categories; a way in which we're dependent on—and limited by—social scripts and norms for guidance, and the way in which these frequently let us down by coming up short when we need them.

That's not to say awkwardness isn't funny, silly, trivial, or sometimes even cute. It's all these things and more. Figuring out how that's possible will take up the first few chapters of the book, because as we'll see, awkwardness is hard to pin down. Perhaps that's fitting, since at its core, it's a response to absence: the absence of social guidance, the absence of a classification.

Being susceptible to awkwardness requires seeing oneself as a being subject to social norms. To be in an awkward situation is to realize simultaneously that you lack guidance and that you should have it; that there's a kind of knowledge you usually have and suddenly don't. Thus, awkwardness requires a kind of social sophistication, and our vulnerability to it is the flipside of our success as social creatures.

This book itself is a bit awkward. My goal is to explain awkwardness and make a case for its philosophical significance, while also gesturing at some practical implications. Because of the nature of the subject, the examples range from serious to silly; I draw on a diverse set of sources. I should also emphasize, to forestall any potential awkwardness, that the examples here, unless attributed to a source, are all fictional. While some may be lightly inspired by my own experiences, no one else is implicated in the anecdotes described here. A second source of awkwardness involves the nature of the project, which attempts to bridge the philosophy and psychology of awkwardness. Most of the existing empirical work (with a few exceptions, which I note as I go) focuses on embarrassment, so where I've co-opted it to apply to awkwardness, I explain how and why.

The structure is as follows: the first two chapters lean toward the descriptive and the empirical, offering a characterization of awkwardness and situating it in relation to similar feelings and experiences. The next four chapters make the normative case for why and where awkwardness matters. After analyzing awkwardness in terms of social scripts in chapter 1, chapter 2 explains what distinguishes feeling awkward from other self-conscious emotions. The remainder of the book assesses awkwardness's normative implications. Chapter 3 looks more closely at the relationship between scripts and social norms, and how both of these guide us through interactions and mark us as insiders or outsiders. In chapter 4, I start to look more closely at the implications of awkwardness for moral discourse. I argue that some problems are morally awkward—they resist categorization in terms of moral, social, or personal issue, complicating our attempts to navigate our obligation. Chapter 5 looks at some ways this ambiguity is exploited—how awkwardness can be "weaponized" to entrench existing forms of power and injustice. But I also show how awkwardness can also be mobilized as a form of resistance. So then, chapter 6 asks, where does this leave us with respect to its normative status? I conclude that chapter—and the book—by offering some suggestions about how to cope with awkwardness: by rewriting our scripts to minimize it where we can, and changing how we experience it and redistributing its costs where we can't.

This is only a start, and it's incomplete. My goal here is not to offer a comprehensive account of awkwardness in all its forms. Rather, it's to make the case for awkwardness as a distinct form of social discomfort worthy of philosophical attention. The book is an attempt at starting a conversation, not the last word. Hopefully, it generates something more than an awkward silence.

Finally, a word of caution is in order: while the book begins by discussing rather trivial, low-stakes cases of awkwardness, I don't mean to suggest that awkwardness itself is trivial. Far from it: as I'll argue throughout the later chapters, awkwardness can be leveraged both to maintain instances of social injustice and exclusion, and to resist them. Part of my hope in writing this book is that by understanding how we get from failed small talk at cocktail parties to failures to hold people accountable for sexual harassment, we will better appreciate the significance of our everyday social interactions, and the opportunities they—and their failures—present. For an experience so often associated with silence, awkwardness has a lot to say.

1
This Is Awkward

1.1 Introduction: What Is Awkward?

This is awkward: you greet an acquaintance you haven't seen for a while. One of you goes in for a hug; the other initially offers a handshake, and then leans in, by which time the hugger is hesitating. In the end, you both do a half-hearted back pat, and then settle into stilted small talk. Variation: suppose the friend is one from whom you've been estranged—your last encounter ended in a falling-out, but that was some time ago, and you haven't spoken since. Does this make things more awkward?

This is awkward, too: you're a graduate student having dinner with a distinguished visiting speaker who wants to hear more about your research. Suddenly, as you're talking, a piece of food flies out of your mouth and lands on their pristine black sweater. Did they see it? Do they know? They must know. But there's no acknowledgment; you try not to stare at it, and continue the interaction, saying nothing.

And this is awkward: someone you consider a friend is engaging in inappropriate flirting at work. They've been going to bars with subordinates after work, and even hooked up with one or two. You think this is sexual harassment, and you know you should talk to them about it, but you can't seem to figure out how to have the conversation.

These examples involve social situations where we find ourselves not knowing how to act. They range from the trivial to the serious, from quick interactions quickly forgotten to longer-term problems with long-term implications. But they're all instances of awkwardness: the thing that happens when we find ourselves in an interaction we don't know how to navigate.

Before proceeding, let me clarify some terminology. "Awkwardness" refers to the property shared by situations like this: the property of being awkward. "Awkward" describes situations that have the property. And then there's feeling awkward, which also sometimes gets referred to with the single term "awkward," or as "awkwardness"—just to complicate things further. When it comes to awkwardness, it can be unclear where it's located and what kind of thing it is—a feeling, a property, or some combination of both. On my account, awkwardness is a property of social interactions, not a feeling (that's why I talk about "feeling awkward," instead of "awkwardness," when describing our inner experience). But it's not surprising that it's hard to determine whether we're describing something internal or external, because when and how a situation becomes awkward depends on our mental states, as well as where we stand in relation to the world, and to each other.

1.2 The Etymology of Awkwardness: How to Get Lost

The relational nature of awkwardness is evident in its etymology: the Old Norse "afgur," meaning "turned the wrong way," becomes the Middle English "awk," meaning "backward," "wrong," or "clumsy." Joining this with the English "ward" yields the literal meaning, "facing the wrong way."[1] This is revealing: not only is the idea of incompetence in the origins of the word, awkwardness is defined in part by how we situate ourselves in relation to our surroundings. The Ancient Greek "skaion," sometimes translated as "clumsy" or "awkward," literally means "from the left hand," and refers to the

---

[1] The discussion of etymology here is informed by Dahl 2018 and Kotsko 2010.

clumsiness of writing originating from our nondominant hand.[2] Here we see the link between literal and social ineptitude, a link further evinced by terms like "maladroit," and other contemporary languages (English but also French, German, and Italian) linking the terms used for "awkward" and "clumsy" or "graceless."[3] But the English word's origins in the idea of facing the wrong way adds an interpersonal element to the idea of clumsy performance: the correct way to face depends in part on where others are facing. It only makes sense to assess someone as facing the wrong way—as awkward—against a background of other social actors. The etymology of the English word, "awkward," is implicitly social. And the property of awkwardness is essentially social, attaching not to individuals or actions in isolation, but emerging out of social interaction, the result of (failed) attempts at coordination.

In another respect though, the etymology is misleading, because while awkward is about being out of sync, it's less about facing the *wrong* way than about not knowing which way to face. Suppose two individuals stand facing one way, waiting for an event to start, and a third arrives and situates themselves facing the other way. One possibility is that the newcomer quickly identifies themselves as in error, and makes this realization known to the others with either an audible admission ("oops, wrong way!") or a facial or postural display of embarrassment (blush; dip of the shoulders or head) as they resituate themselves. In this case, the situation is reorganized and resolved via the newcomer's acknowledgment of error.

Another possibility is that the newcomer doesn't resituate themselves. Now the two others may be unsure: why not? Does the

---

[2] I'm not suggesting this term would have all or even most of the contemporary connotations of awkwardness; my colleague Justin Clark brought the translation to my attention. Harré (1990) claims that the ancient Greeks lack a word for our contemporary emotion of embarrassment, which suggests they would likely think of awkwardness differently as well, perhaps drawing a tighter conceptual link between physical awkwardness and character than we do today—although, as we'll see in chapter 3, we also make this inference sometimes.

[3] For example, the French "maladroit"; the German terms "unangenhem," "unbeholfen," and "ungeschickt"; and the Italian "sgraziato."

newcomer know something they don't? Should they correct them? Might they be the ones in error? (If this example seems too abstract, consider a case where you're attending a yoga class for the first time and you're not sure where to put your mat.)

It may seem like I'm making a mountain out of an etymological molehill here, but the imagery of direction is an apt illustration of some features of awkwardness, and a useful starting point for our discussion. Awkwardness isn't a matter of being in the wrong, or being different—it's about the uncertainty of not knowing how to react in situations where we find ourselves wrong, or different. Situations become awkward when interactants aren't sure how to adjust to one another's behavior. As we'll see shortly, our behavior is often guided by norms and scripts. Where these are absent or unclear, we have to improvise at the speed of social interaction. That's complicated, partly because how we make such adjustments is determined by the perceived status, knowledge, and social orientation of those around us—information we don't always have.

In the next few sections, I elaborate on the idea that awkwardness is the result of ambiguous or absent social guidance. I start by describing some existing analyses of awkwardness, on which my account builds. I then detour into the concept of social scripts. Scripts are a significant source of social guidance, and appreciating their role helps us understand how and why awkwardness happens.

1.3 Making It Awkward: Sources of Awkwardness in Everyday Life

Awkwardness can be the result of novel or unfamiliar social situations, but it also arises in the course of relatively mundane activities, like walking down the sidewalk. Most of us have had the experience of trying to pass someone on the street when both of you feint the same way, and then correct by simultaneously feinting the other way. It's slightly awkward, though usually benign. What's striking is how often it doesn't happen: most of the time, we navigate sidewalks just fine. Likewise, we coordinate joint activities and commitments with little explicit conversation and effort.[4] The failed sidewalk pass highlights the fluency with which we usually pass through the social world; awkwardness offers a kind of "insight through breakdown" (Kotsko 2010: 15).

Kotsko's description evokes the social dysfunction that characterizes awkwardness. Avoiding it isn't just a matter of having social skills; it requires the right match between actor, skill, and environment. Kotsko describes awkwardness as what happens when the norms we usually depend on—without even realizing it, perhaps—are suddenly absent, unavailable, or inadequate. He analyzes variations of awkwardness ranging from the "everyday"—involving gaffes and violations of "known social norms"—to "cultural" awkwardness, in which there are norms in play but "it feels somehow impossible to follow them or even fully know them."

But normative failure alone doesn't suffice for awkwardness. It's not just being wrong that manifests incompetence—it's the failure to get things back on track. When we violate a social norm or commit a gaffe, we fall short as individuals. That's embarrassing. (More on that in the next chapter.) But failing to coordinate one's actions with others around you is awkward—for you and for them. In his book on embarrassment, Miller describes awkwardness as "emerge[ing] from the combined behavior of two or more people, all of them individually blameless ... an *interaction* becomes awkward" (1996: 61, emphasis on "interaction" mine). Clegg's description of awkwardness as a kind of "social destabilization" is apt in this respect, since being destabilized implies a difficulty in regaining one's balance (2012a, 2012b). As we saw earlier, we often orient and stabilize ourselves by looking to others for cues. Sometimes those cues are ambiguous, absent, or inscrutable. When that happens, coordination fails—and things get awkward.

---

[4] See Gilbert's discussion of going for a walk together in her 1990.

This isn't a full explanation of awkwardness—not yet. And it might be hard to see how this works in practice to explain the breakdown of more complex interactions. Think back to the examples with which we started: running into an estranged friend at a party and not knowing how to interact with them; accidentally spitting food onto a colleague's sweater at dinner. How are these like a simple case of not knowing where to physically position oneself? Here it might seem that self-presentation, rather than coordination, is the issue. But knowing which self to bring to the occasion, and how to present that self, requires coordinating with other people's knowledge and expectations. For example: does the other person know they have food on them? Do they know that you know? Do they expect an apology, or are they happy to pretend everything's fine? Is everything actually fine? Without answers to these questions, successfully navigating one of these situations—bringing the right "self," and performing the right actions—can seem like an impossible task.

1.4 Awkwardness and Etiquette

Social interactions, and the split-second decisions they require, demand that we navigate complex issues involving others' knowledge and desires quickly and fluently, while occupying a carefully calibrated physical space, distance, and posture. Putting too much thought into any of this will not only make it look less effortless, it will throw off the timing of our speech and movement, which in turn will throw off our interlocutor's speech and movement, making things (you guessed it) awkward. Taking all this into account, the puzzle is less about how things become awkward than about how things are ever *not* awkward. Our reliance on infrastructure is most evident when that infrastructure fails. So: what's the infrastructure that facilitates social coordination and whose failure makes things awkward?

One candidate is etiquette. We tend to think of etiquette as a concern played out in formal social settings, but it's all around us—as Stohr (2018: 719) points out, "there is no such thing as an etiquette-free zone." It may be more salient in formal settings, but that's partly a function of their specialness: the occasions that require us to think about etiquette stand out precisely because they're not ones we encounter every day. That doesn't mean our everyday manners are any less real. A traveler might be more likely than a local to notice the norms governing behavior on public transportation, simply because unfamiliar norms are more salient—and more effortful to follow. But part of what it is to "have" manners is to internalize the rules of good etiquette, and it's in this internalization that the real benefit lies. The rules of etiquette reduce the cognitive burden of everyday life; because of them, in social situations, "the work of deciding what to do happens elsewhere" (Olberding 2016: 440).

We can contrast formal, rule-based systems of etiquette with the less formalized, more general category of manners. Olberding (2019: 30–31) writes that "manners concern how we navigate the low-level, low-stakes, commonplace interactions of everyday life." Our preoccupation with manners is more than snobbery: it's part of what it is to be social. As Goffman observes, "societies everywhere, if they are to be societies, must mobilize their members as self-regulating participants in social encounters" (1967: 44). The norms of etiquette are one way we do this; violating or disregarding them is, literally, antisocial.

Etiquette expresses respect and acknowledges our commitment to one another. Practicing good manners helps regulate our tendencies to express and even to feel morally problematic emotions such as contempt and disgust; it makes us attentive to the presence, needs, and expectations of others. Olberding compares the effect to choreography: "The prescribed steps protect coparticipants in the dance of social intercourse, averting conflicts. . . . Minimally, the rules encode deference to the constraints of shared social space;

maximally, they enable cooperative and collaborative accord" (2016: 429). Like a skillful dance, navigating conversational pauses, physical proximity, and eye contact is done best when it appears effortless; good manners guide and are realized in successful performances.

A person who refuses to play their role can bring down the whole show. Rudeness is not just hostile; it's threatening. To be rude requires knowing what etiquette demands and then refusing to accede. Awkwardness is different. It manifests ignorance, incompetence, or both. Compare the distinction between lying and bullshit: the liar has to acknowledge the truth, and pay it a kind of respect, in order to lie in the first place. The bullshitter can sail right past it. Similarly, rudeness acknowledges etiquette even as it refuses to comply.[5] Awkwardness doesn't. Someone who makes things awkward isn't being defiant; they can't defy the rules, because they don't "have" them. (The analogy isn't perfect: unlike the bullshitter, the awkward person might care very much about the rules, but be unable to know and follow them.)

But etiquette is only part of the answer. To know what manners to bring to the table, I have to locate an occasion in the space of events: is it a dinner party or a wedding? Until I can answer these questions, etiquette can't begin to guide me. Identifying the relevant norms requires narrowing down the space of possible events, and locating one's social position and role within that space. The category of infrastructure we're looking for is both broader and informationally richer than either the rules of etiquette or the less formal guidance of manners. What we need is a social script.

---

[5] One could argue that it's possible to be unintentionally rude. But I don't think so; this would be like unintentionally lying—it's not a lie; it's a mistake.

1.5 Awkwardness: Socializing Unscripted

Scripts are "the central guiding tool for coordinating behaviors in social interactions" that "tell people how to interact in different situational and cultural contexts" (Eickers 2023: 86). They're "generic knowledge structures" for events: "prescriptive sequences of actions . . . that people automatically engage in (and are expected to engage in) while in particular situations" (Bicchieri 2016: 132). Note the word "prescriptive": scripts include norms as well as elements like roles and behaviors. For example, the restaurant script includes normative elements like "leave a tip" and "treat the waiter with courtesy." But even apparently descriptive elements are normative insofar as someone departing from them violates our expectations and may be met with disapproval.

The term "script" is used with varying degrees of breadth. Early discussions treat scripts as akin to computer programs: a way to organize socially relevant information and store it "off-line," where it can be called up as needed to fill in gaps in social cues and guide us through events (Schank & Abelson 1977; Abelson 1981). Contemporary work analyzes scripts as "schemata for events," for example, the "dinner party script" or the "CEO leading a meeting" script (Bicchieri & McNally 2018). The term is also used in a broader sense, to pick out the way we situate and understand an experience—the beliefs and normative appraisals we associate with it—as when we talk about scripts for grief, or anxiety.[6]

Scripts are tools for social coordination: they function only if they're shared and accepted by sufficiently many members of the relevant group. But acceptance is different from endorsement. I might find myself performing the "caring and nurturing professor" script despite rejecting the expectations placed on women faculty compared to men. This is less puzzling than it initially

---

[6] For discussion, see Munch-Jurisic 2021 and Eickers & Prinz 2020. I come back to this point in chapter 5.

seems. On the assumption that scripts are something I use to guide my individual behaviors and judgments, it seems odd that I would consent to a script whose normative underpinnings I reject. But this individualistic picture of scripts is flawed; scripts are better understood not as guiding individual behavior, but as coordinating group behavior.[7] Once we understand it this way, we can see why we conform to scripts—and feel pressure to conform to them—even when they're suboptimal or downright problematic.

The examples of a dinner party or meeting involve scripts as setting out our conscious expectations for individuals and events. But scripts can also operate beneath conscious awareness, triggered by subtle features of an interaction. We can think of factors like conversational timing, gaze direction, or physical posture as cues that activate scripts: how far away someone stands; how long they hold a gaze, or the conversational floor, is a signal about what kind of interaction we're engaged in. For example, "turn-taking" is a universal feature of human conversation that emerges early in development. Patterns of speech are relatively stable and predictable, with most turns lasting roughly two seconds and pauses between turns usually lasting around 200 ms—about the length of a single syllable (Levinson 2016).[8]

The upshot is that when a speaker or an exchange diverges from these patterns, things can get awkward. We've all had the experience of a conversation where both parties start to speak at the same time, then pause, then start to speak simultaneously again. This can be awkward—the verbal equivalent of a failed sidewalk pass. Conversation requires coordination, and we depend on certain regularities that allow us to project and anticipate others' utterances (and their timing) before they happen, which in turn allows us to time our own interjections.

---

[7] For extended discussion of this point, see Eickers & Prinz 2020.
[8] Though Enfield notes that the pause in turn-taking can vary considerably cross-culturally, with northern Scandinavia being "excruciatingly slow" (2017: 57).

This is a generalization, of course. Part of what's interesting about timing patterns is that they carry normative information, but what that information is depends on the type of conversation and the speakers' identities, roles, and attitudes. For example, the meaning of interruption differs across cultural "scripts" for conversation and depending on the speaker: sometimes it conveys enthusiasm and active listening; other times, disrespect and disengagement (Murata 1994; Tannen 1981). For example, Margaret Thatcher's interviews have been described as having "an awkwardness about them because of the fact that she was often interrupted." Enfield (2017: 45) attributes this to her unusual patterns of intonation, a drop in tone that led hearers to mistakenly conclude she was finishing a turn. Beattie et al. (1982) point out that Thatcher's speech is also distinguished by a refusal to cede the conversational turn, and to make her point even if it requires prolonged periods of "simultaneous speech," which leads to an awkward amount of conversational overlap. The authors' puzzlement as to why Thatcher seems so "domineering," refusing to cede her conversational turn even as she's so frequently interrupted, illustrates yet another point about scripts, which we'll return to in chapters 3 and 5: they depend not only on culture, but on the identities of the actors.

Conversations marked by unintended cross-talk or protracted conversational pauses don't just sound bad, they feel bad. Conversational disfluency can leave participants feeling stressed and rejected (Koudenberg et al. 2011). Mismatched conversational scripts can not only make things awkward in terms of timing, but lead to negative inferences about others' attitudes—inferences we may not even know we're making. And our desire to avoid awkward conversations may involve coalescing on scripts that don't reflect anyone's preferences. For example, studies suggest that in many cases, conversational partners would both prefer a conversation to go on longer, but (falsely) believe that their interlocutor doesn't, so both parties end up in a shorter exchange than they'd prefer (Kardas et al. 2022). This may avoid awkward situations, but at the expense of depriving us of potentially enjoyable and meaningful social contact. In sum, an awkward silence is awkward in part because we don't know what it signifies, and it leaves us without cues about where to go next.

The case of conversational timing is one instance where we might not be able to pinpoint *why* a conversation feels awkward, or "off." Another is gaze: we're sensitive both to the direction in which someone's looking when they talk to us, and for how long. Typically, people look at our face while we're talking; talking with someone who looks just to the left or right, or who doesn't look in our eyes at all, is unnerving—but so is talking with someone who maintains constant, unbroken eye contact (Kleinke 1986; Argyle et al. 1974). Likewise, someone who stands just a bit closer than we're used to when conversing might come across as awkward, because we're unable to pinpoint what feels wrong about the interaction. There's a difference between someone who stands threateningly close and someone who stands awkwardly close: in the first case, we know what the distance conveys, and how we are supposed to react (by backing down or stepping up); in the second case, we're unclear on both counts.

In fact, physical distance during conversation is cross-culturally variable, and calibrated depending on our relationship and the social context: proxemics—the study of social space and interpersonal distance—divides distances into intimate, personal, social, and public.[9] But how these distinctions are defined in practice may vary depending on culture, so the possibilities for error multiply: standing at a public distance from my date feels awkward; standing closer than an "American" personal distance might feel comfortable for someone from the Middle East, but awkward to a New Yorker (Kreuz & Roberts 2017).

---

[9] Hall (1968) originates the term; see also Argyle (1990) for this and other forms of nonverbal communication.

1.6 Awkwardness and Deviance

Scripts are flexible to allow for the possible variations on a situation (if the meal is served buffet-style, if the class is taking an exam).[10] Some deviations from the norm are "built-in," and we accommodate them. Others are unexpected and throw us off-kilter. For example, my script for teaching a class includes norms about student respect, attention, seating location, dress, and posture. But if a student is texting during class, dozing off, or snickering while another student speaks, I'm not totally thrown. These are predictable, even scripted, forms of deviance, and I have my responses ready-to-hand. This isn't true for everyone, and it explains why it can be hard to adjust to teaching at different institutions: what counts as a violation—and how to respond—differs depending on the prevailing local scripts. As we'll see in chapter 3, awkwardness often functions to distinguish insiders and outsiders: because scripts aren't usually formally transmitted, knowing the relevant expectations and how to respond to deviations is a marker of belonging.

The form of deviance involved is part of what distinguishes awkwardness from embarrassment (I'll elaborate on this difference in the next chapter). Some forms of deviance are more predictable than others, and our scripts can anticipate these; it's the unscripted deviations that tend to lead to awkwardness. Going back to the restaurant script example, a server who takes significantly longer than expected to arrive and take an order represents a deviation from the script, but a predictable one; when this happens, our scripted response is annoyance, frustration, or anger. On the other hand, a server who bursts into tears while taking our order may leave us feeling confused and, yes, awkward, because this is an unexpected deviation from the script and we're not sure how to respond. Miller (1996: 61) gives the example of a phone call becoming awkward

---

[10] In this respect, scripts are more like Daston's (2022) "thick" rules: flexible and able to accommodate/tolerate exceptions.

when one party starts to suspect that the other has romantic intentions. At this point, two things happen: it's unclear what type of conversation is happening, making it hard for either party to locate and follow the relevant script, and it's also unclear how to get the conversation back onto friendly ground without explicitly acknowledging and rejecting the romantic overtures, which in turn will make things uncomfortable. The example incorporates a number of themes that will recur throughout the book: the way awkwardness emerges from discoordinated interactions, but also the way that norms about discomfort and who should manage it tend to disadvantage some groups over others, the way politeness can prevent us from explicitly acknowledging certain topics (out of fear of making it awkward), the way situations impose roles upon us, even when we prefer not to play them.

The script for the phone call becomes ambiguous when the two parties are suspected to have different intentions or desires. In other cases, it's not the parties themselves but features of the situation that create ambiguity about which script to follow. A simple example involves the rapid rise of screen-based payment processors, which often automatically offer the option to add a gratuity. Compounding the anxiety is the fact that the customer is choosing a tip while the staffer watches. Sometimes this is unproblematic and familiar: buying a latte in a coffeeshop. But when businesses fill two or more roles—a retail shop that also operates as a café; a record store that serves coffee—things can get awkward, as a customer buying a jar of tahini or a stack of records is confronted with a tipping option. On the one hand, social norms tell us we don't tip on ordinary retail transactions, but the presence of the tip option suggests that we should. Here, technology creates ambiguity about which script we are following. It may also create truly novel situations for which there is no script.

Awkwardness is a disruption in our social performance and navigation. But it's not just any kind of disruption. After all, we violate social norms frequently, and react to violations in all kinds of ways—amusement, annoyance, offense, anger. Why should some specific subset turn into awkwardness? The answer involves distinguishing disruptions consisting of the violation of social norms from disruptions resulting from the absence of a script: the former might give rise to annoyance, or embarrassment, or amusement; the latter might give rise to awkwardness. Both can send a social interaction off-track, but the remedies are different. In the case of rudeness, for example, we have to find a way to rebuke the person, or ignore them. The professor facing a rude student must find a way to keep the lecture "on script," just as a host facing a rude dinner party guest must signal to other guests that the party will proceed. The remedy for awkwardness is different: it makes no sense to offer a rebuke; what the situation demands is a lifeline. This explains the phenomenological distinction between awkwardness and other forms of self-conscious emotions like guilt, shame, and embarrassment: as we'll see in chapter 2, these are scripted emotional responses to norm violations; awkwardness is unscripted.

There's a functional logic to awkwardness and the feelings that accompany it. We tend to focus on norm violations, but the absence of normative guidance can have just as significant an impact on our social lives. A rich emotional repertoire underwrites moral and social norms, kicking in when we violate—or even contemplate violating—them. So, I feel guilty about telling a white lie; I feel ashamed of my failure to bring a gift; I feel embarrassed by my lack of preparation for the talk. What's missing from this list is an affective reaction to not having a norm when we need one. What's the feeling that makes us seek out the guidance of social norms in the first place? And what's the feeling that kicks in to let us know we're lacking it? The aversiveness of awkward experience motivates us to coordinate, and the salience (both in the moment and in our memories) of awkwardness highlights areas where our social guidance is insufficient or absent.

1.7 This Is Awkward: An Analysis

Awkwardness is a property that characterizes social situations or interactions when one or more participant(s) finds themselves lacking the guidance of a script and feels awkward as a result. This can happen for a number of reasons: we don't recognize the situation we're in, or the environment doesn't cue a script for us; we realize we are uncoordinated (with other interactants); we are uncertain about which role is ours or how to play it; we lack the capacity, either material, physical, or epistemic to play the role. Goffman (1956: 265) writes that "there is no social encounter which cannot become embarrassing," and the same might be said for awkwardness. So I won't catalog every way we might find ourselves lacking a script. The possibilities are vast. Nor is my goal here to define awkwardness in terms of necessary and sufficient conditions. Instead, I offer a general characterization, which I'll flesh out in more detail in the remainder of this chapter.

As I explain below, we can distinguish awkwardness as a property from the feelings that accompany it. If awkwardness is the property, "awkward" describes things that have that property. So, throughout the book, I'll talk about "awkward situations," or describe things as "being awkward." By this I mean a situation where awkwardness occurs, or a situation that gives rise to awkwardness. I say more about this in section 1.8 below, but a situation is awkward if it has the property of awkwardness; an issue, subject, or conversation is awkward if engaging with it gives rise to the property of awkwardness.

Whether or not a situation is awkward depends on the people involved. A conversation about sex isn't awkward, full stop—it's awkward to have with your parents. The reason for that has to do with the expectations around the role of "parent," and the way it intersects with our attitudes toward sex. I'll return to the interplay between norms, roles, and scripts in chapters 3 and 4, but for now note how awkwardness shifts depending on the individuals and contexts involved. It's a moving target: as our attitudes and expectations change, subjects become more or less awkward. For example, as we shift our attitudes toward salary, viewing it less as an indicator of our own self-worth and more of an issue of justice and equity, conversations about salary become less awkward. Again, I say more about this later, specifically in chapter 6, where I discuss ways of rewriting our social scripts.

Most of us can recall examples of awkwardness more vividly than we'd like. While the details can vary, there are some common elements to the feelings involved in awkward experiences. Specifically, I'll argue that there are three related but distinct components of feeling awkward: uncertainty, self-consciousness, and discomfort. In the next section, I say more about the phenomenology of awkwardness and explain how feeling awkward relates to the property of awkwardness.

1.7.1 Awkward Feelings

Perhaps the most salient aspect of awkwardness is that it's uncomfortable. In fact, it is tempting to think that discomfort exhausts the phenomenology of awkwardness. That's partly because discomfort is broad enough that it can seem to encompass various other aspects of awkwardness. I'll say more about discomfort and the other affective elements of awkward feelings in chapter 2, but the short version is, discomfort alone isn't sufficient for feeling awkward: uncertainty and self-consciousness are also involved.

Being unsure about what to do, say, or how to act is an essential element of feeling awkward. Uncertainty isn't always aversive: sometimes it's exciting, or arousing. But in the case of feeling awkward, we're not in suspense; we're at a loss for what to do next. The breakdown of our social script means that our usual give-and-take is interrupted, and we can't rely on it for guidance. And our usual social cues, be they explicit or implicit, are absent or insufficient to get us back on track. So, we feel frozen, and the longer this uncertainty persists, the more awkward things get.

Another salient aspect of awkward feelings is self-consciousness. Clegg (2012a: 267) interviewed undergraduate subjects about their experiences of awkwardness. They described "intense, focused, social attention" and "heightened awareness . . . of self and others." This focus only compounds the feeling of awkwardness. Awkwardness draws attention to what are usually automatic or unreflective behaviors; this, in turn, gives rise to increased self-monitoring. (Incidentally, I think this explains why being stoned often feels awkward: not because we don't know how we're supposed to act, but because we're constantly and intensely wondering whether we're actually pulling it off.

These feelings—discomfort, uncertainty, and self-consciousness—distinguish awkward situations from other instances where we find ourselves without a script. For example, suppose I am actually lost, but intentionally so—I set out to find a strange environment and disorient myself, or take hallucinogenic drugs that put me in a state of euphoria. In these cases, I have no expectation of knowing how to act, thus my lack of script seems not just predictable but acceptable. Through no choice of my own, I might find myself in a situation for which I lack a script and become frustrated by that fact, or scared. Lacking a script can be fun, too: Ridge (2021) argues that unscriptedness is one of the defining characteristics of play, a paradigmatically enjoyable activity.[11] Compare this to the situation where I find myself without a script—or find myself with multiple scripts, unsure which to choose—and become self-conscious, uncertain, and uncomfortable: that's awkward.

---

[11] Though I do think play can feel awkward; I've had the experience of playing with children, including my own, and feeling awkward. One might argue that this shows I wasn't really succeeding at play, and I think that's a fair point.

This raises the question of how *feeling* awkward relates to awkwardness: can one feel awkward without being awkward? It's complicated. On the one hand, yes: awkwardness requires both the lack of script and the awkward feelings that result. But it's not necessary that all the parties to the interaction have those feelings—that's part of why awkwardness lends itself to problematic manipulation, as we'll see. As the examples of play, drug-taking, and frustration show, you can also have unscriptedness without awkward feelings, in which case you have something else, not awkwardness. Lastly, it's possible to have awkward feelings but not actually lack a script. In this case, it would be incorrect to say the situation was awkward, though one could still correctly report *feeling* awkward. But mistakes about whether a situation is awkward are going to be less common than mistakes about, say, whether a situation is sad, because the feature that makes a situation awkward—namely, our ability to rely on scripts for social guidance—is more directly accessible to us than the features that make a situation sad, for example, or enviable. In the next section, I look more closely at how awkwardness arises; in chapter 2, I'll say more about feeling awkward.

1.7.2 Off-Script: Awkward Interactions

What's special about *social* scripts is their interpersonal, coordinative function: they help us figure out not only what we should do, but how to make sense of other people's behaviors, intentions, and roles. For a script to accomplish this purpose, we need to know what we're doing (or intending, or believing), what other people are doing (or intending, or believing), and who other people are being—a boss versus a friend; a potential romantic partner versus a helpful stranger. For a script to fail, it can be enough that we're not sure what situation we're in (is it a date?), which role we're playing (are we friends, or colleagues?), or what our line is supposed to be (am I criticizing or helping?). When I talk about lacking a script,

I mean it in an individual, functional sense—we don't have a script to get us through the current situation. I don't necessarily mean that we are, as a society, without one—although that's also possible. In later chapters, I discuss cases where we collectively lack scripts for engaging in certain kinds of conversations or talking about certain issues.

Because scripts encode a variety of information, there are a number of ways they can fail. Thus, the various elements of scripts—roles, norms, behaviors, speech—are all potential sources of awkwardness. Goffman's (1959) model of self-presentation as performance offers one story about how the selves we inhabit depend on scripts, and can conflict or prove inadequate for the script at hand, thus producing awkwardness. In ordinary circumstances, I have different selves which I perform for different occasions and—more importantly—different audiences. But occasionally one of my selves is forced to make an appearance before an audience which usually witnesses a different self. In these cases, "individuals confront one another with selves incompatible with the ones they extend to each other on different occasions" (1956: 269). A character on the TV show *My So-Called Life* sums it up well: "What I, like, dread is when people who know you in completely different ways end up in the same area. And you have to develop this, like, combination you on the spot" (quoted in King 2021). Figuring out which self to bring to a given situation is partly a matter of knowing and activating the correct social script; without a script to guide us, we're forced to improvise, each looking to the other as we try to coordinate.

As we'll see, scripts fail for any number of reasons. Earlier, I referred to Goffman's observation that there is no situation that cannot become embarrassing, which is almost right. In fact, there's virtually no situation that cannot become awkward, since our scripts can fail to coordinate us for so many reasons: a behavior so unexpected that it makes us question the script in play; something makes us unsure about which role we're playing within a script;

we need to perform a task (have a conversation, take up a physical stance/position, convey a feeling or commitment) that's incompatible with the script we're currently engaged with. Sometimes we just don't know how to engage in a behavior or conversation. I'll return to strategies for ameliorating awkwardness at the end of the book, but note that one strategy for handling difficult conversations is to offer people actual, literal scripts: either behaviors or conversational openers they can use to raise potentially awkward topics like relationship issues, mental health, and sex.[12]

The most familiar and obvious form of awkwardness involves cases where we find ourselves totally without a script: we don't know what to do or say (this is similar to Kotsko's "radical awkwardness," mentioned above). This might happen because a situation is so novel that there isn't a social script to guide us through it. Does the gestational surrogate get invited to the baby shower? Is it weird if your boss likes your Instagram posts? Technological and social advances create situations for which we lack widely known and agreed-upon norms: the increasing social visibility of polyamory; the use of "gig labor" such as Taskrabbit and Instacart; teaching classes on Zoom. These and other innovations have, in some cases, outpaced the development of social norms guiding their application and governance. One strategy is to borrow from existing scripts: taking the familiar concept of anxiety and using it as a characterization of postpartum experience to yield the concept of "postpartum anxiety." This offers not only a new clinical diagnosis, but a new way of relating to one's experiences, a point I return to in chapter 5. Individually, we sometimes approach an unfamiliar event by borrowing from or modifying a more familiar script: adding a request for students' pronouns at the same time we ask them to introduce themselves (I come back to this example in chapter 6).

---

[12] For example, public health campaigns like seizetheawkward.org offer strategies for broaching conversations about mental health.

We often end up without a script when we're in unfamiliar territory, whether literally or figuratively: another country, another religion's rituals. However, in these cases we know to expect unfamiliarity; awkwardness prefers to sneak up on us. More mundane scenarios also sometimes present challenges. For example, what to do at a party where you don't know anyone? We know how to make conversation; we know how to pour a drink, or get food. But when these familiar options fail us, what then? What do we do at a conference when no one speaks to us and we can't make an exit? These are not the kind of dilemmas philosophers usually concern themselves with; the stakes here seem low, petty even. But they can be painfully awkward nonetheless—and especially where others' performance seems effortless, our failures can mark us as outsiders.

1.7.3 Awkward Hesitation

Scripts involve coordination with others, so one cause of awkwardness is being unsure about the status of a piece of knowledge: whether to explicitly acknowledge something everyone knows, thereby bringing it out into the open. A workplace affair, tension in a friendship, an overheard but unacknowledged criticism—any of these can make an interaction awkward, by creating ambiguity about what's being treated as common knowledge. Bringing something out into the open—even if it's already staring everyone in the face—creates a demand for acknowledgment, which can make things more, rather than less, awkward.

For example, imagine you're walking across campus with a visiting job candidate after a recent snowstorm, and pass the work of some creative students: a six-foot-tall, anatomically correct penis, sculpted out of snow. Do you acknowledge its presence? You could risk a joke, but the norm is not to joke about genitalia with job candidates. On the other hand, one doesn't usually find oneself confronted with snow sculptures of genitalia when walking with job candidates, so does this license an exception to the norm? It's awkward because obviously you both see the thing, so not remarking on it leaves the status of this piece of knowledge unresolved: there's something I know you know, and you know I know, and yet we're not commenting on it. Or take a more familiar experience: you're watching a movie with your parents when a sex scene comes on the screen. If no one says anything to acknowledge the discomfort, it quickly becomes awkward.[13] Alternatively, someone could make a joke or comment about how uncomfortable things are, which potentially defuses the awkwardness.

In these cases, we're unsure how to locate one another with respect to the subject. The ambiguity resides both in the status of the knowledge involved and in our relationship: do we have the kind of relationship that means we're comfortable discussing this? Am I in a position where I can comment on my boss's relationships, or make a joke about the giant snow sculpture? The importance of mutual knowledge (or acknowledgment) in making these calculations shows that it's not just roles, but relationships, that determine which scripts are available to us in any given situation: uncertainty about how we're relating to others in a given moment leads to uncertainty about which script to follow.

There are (at least) two potential pitfalls in choosing between scripts: first, we might choose the wrong script by picking one that's inappropriate. If I'm unsure whether to shake hands or hug, and I opt to go in for a hug, I might immediately recognize my mistake based on the other person's reaction. Alternatively, the problem might not be that my choice is inappropriate, but that it's not coordinated: I go in for a hug, but he holds out a hand for shaking. Here, I've also chosen wrongly, but what makes the action wrong isn't the choice per se, it's that it misaligns with his choice. Recall the point

---

[13] In a 2022 yougov.com poll, this was the second-most frequently cited example of an awkward situation. Number one? "Accidentally sending a gossipy message to the subject of the gossip" (Orth 2022).

above: scripts are a way to anticipate and coordinate with others' actions; if I choose an action that is misaligned, there's a sense in which I chose the wrong script, but there's also a sense in which I have no script at all. An analogy with games might help here: if I sit down at the board of black and white squares and start moving chess pieces, and you sit across from me and start moving checkers, there's a sense in which we're playing two different games, but really, we're not playing any game at all. The same holds for scripts: when I go in for a professional handshake, and you go in for a hug, we're not enacting a script, because we're not coordinating; we've failed to anticipate and triangulate on a set of actions and reactions. Scripts' role in coordinating social interactions shows that lacking a script isn't just an individual problem: if I don't know which script we're performing, we both lack a script, because your ability to perform depends in part on mine.

Ambiguity about which script is in play can throw off the flow of social interaction for all involved, creating awkwardness. And this fact about ambiguity lends itself to abuse; as I'll argue later on, people can and do leverage awkwardness as a way to manipulate or subjugate others. Putting someone in an ambiguous situation and thereby making them feel awkward is one way to do this: when someone is in an awkward situation, they badly want to resolve it, and that makes them vulnerable; they may feel pressure to accept the scripts offered them in order to reduce discomfort (not just their own, but others' discomfort as well). We'll discuss this in more detail in chapter 5, when we talk about awkwardness and injustice.

Finally, it's worth noting that awkwardness isn't fixed in place; while some issues or topics or conversations may lend themselves to awkwardness in virtue of their normative complexity, the boundaries of awkwardness shift as issues become more familiar and more scripted. And the speed of social media lets us negotiate issues more quickly, disseminating scripts and terminology with which to discuss them—a point I discuss in chapter 6.

1.8 Everything Is Awkward

The discussion so far might give the impression that awkwardness looms constantly. According to the analysis I've offered, though, awkwardness is an essentially social property, so it seems that only social interactions or situations can be awkward. This seems to require revising ordinary talk about awkwardness: we use "awkward" to describe physical gestures or movements; the placement of furniture; the plating of a dish of food. Is this a problem? Put another way, is my account too revisionary of our everyday usage?

There are a few different replies to this. First, the analysis actually covers more than we might expect; we can talk about things like awkward silences (or awkward plates of food) in terms of their ambiguous signification. Not all silences are awkward: they can be profound or companionable. Pauses can be pregnant. Sometimes we know exactly what a silence means, and what it demands: silences can be full of meaning. But they can also be ambiguous or confusing. Those are the awkward silences: the ones that leave us uncertain. Like conversational pauses and silences, objects can be awkward if they throw us off-course, leaving us unsure of how to proceed.

The plate of food may present itself as confusing or ambiguous if it doesn't offer enough cues: do I cut into it? Pick it up with my fingers? This uncertainty can transfer to our behaviors, making them awkward, too: there's a difference between the person who confidently picks up the food with her fingers (rude, maybe?) and the person who hesitantly pokes at it (awkward). Physical actions present as awkward if we see them as reflecting a lack of savoir faire; where someone's behavior or posture is uncertain, we ourselves aren't sure what they're trying to do, and this makes them an unreliable partner in action (more about this in chapter 3). So, to say that something is awkward is to say that it doesn't fit into a social category, either because it's ambiguous or because it defies classification.

A second line of response involves pointing to other cases where we use psychological or emotion terms metaphorically. "Disgusting" functions this way sometimes: we use it to amplify and underline our judgments, without meaning to literally convey nauseated revulsion.[14] When we describe someone as "disgustingly good at football," it's not because we're confused about the meaning of the word. Describing the positioning of a couch, or the phrasing of a sentence, as awkward can similarly be understood either as metaphor or amplifier.[15] Ultimately, the relationship between "theoretical" and ordinary uses of psychological terms involves a trade-off. Sometimes, we invoke a clinical term in a colloquial sense with a kind of winking sensibility: when we call someone a psychopath, or refer to someone as a clinical narcissist, we know we're not applying the label correctly; that's part of the colloquial appeal.

However, there is one counterintuitive implication of my account: I think that there are no awkward people, only awkward interactions. This may strike some readers as unacceptably revisionary. Virtually everyone either thinks they know an especially awkward person, or self-identifies as one. But this is wrong: awkwardness or "being awkward" is not a property of individuals. That's partly a consequence of the metaphysics of awkwardness: it's a property of social interactions, not people. While some people may be more prone to awkward feelings, or to evoking those feelings in others, that is not the same as being awkward itself. In the next section, I explain why.

---

[14] There's controversy about whether *all* verbal expressions of moral disgust are metaphorical in this sense (see Chapman & Anderson 2013). Regardless of where one stands on that issue, it's clear that some expressions are metaphorical. I don't intend to prejudge that debate here, just to point out that we have no trouble accepting some figurative language in the disgust case.

[15] In the case of disgust, I think we find both types of nonliteral use, and I expect the same can be said about awkwardness. Here, my goal isn't to make the case for one of these over the other, or even to argue about how to distinguish them—merely to point out that there are various ways to accommodate nonliteral uses of psychological descriptions. For discussion of the distinction in the disgust case, see Fileva 2020 and May 2018.

1.9 There Are No Awkward People, Only Awkward Situations

Our use of "awkward" to describe people is ambiguous. Sometimes, it's used to describe someone whose behavior suggests that they're feeling awkward—"he's been awkward with me ever since the breakup." In other cases, it's used to describe someone whose behavior causes others to feel awkward. These come apart—a person's failure to make eye contact might make me feel awkward, even if they have no such feeling. And in some cases, a single description can be interpreted either way: "she's awkward at parties" can be read as suggesting that she feels awkward at parties, or that she makes other people feel awkward at parties. And both can be true—the ambiguity stems in part from the fact that other people's discomfort can make us uncomfortable, so that being around someone who's feeling awkward can make us feel awkward, too. Finally, we sometimes blame people for awkwardness not because they've caused it, but because they could resolve it, but don't—the person who lets an awkward silence hang, or who fails to engage in small talk. The point is that our meanings and intuitions here are often unclear. Where our practice is confused to begin with, a little revision may not be a bad thing; where that confusion allows bias to creep in, revision is good.

Despite all this, it does seem like some people are more prone to awkwardness than others. This isn't just an observation from the outside: people often self-report feeling awkward, or talking about certain times in their life as awkward, or just describing themselves as awkward. First, some individuals occupy a kind of liminal social status. Since awkwardness is caused by a lack of social script, people who don't fit easily into a social role—or who sit uneasily at the juncture of more than one—might be especially prone to awkward situations. For example, teenagers occupy a liminal position: sort-of-children, sort-of-adults. As teenagers, we're acquiring social norms from our peers while becoming enculturated into adult roles—in other words, it's a time of rapid horizontal social learning.[16] It's also a time when we're particularly prone to awkwardness.

Some people may also have difficulty taking social cues from conversational timing, gaze, or physical proximity. For example, Tashiro frames his book on the psychology of awkwardness around his own experiences as a self-described "socially awkward" child. For Tashiro, "being awkward," or "being an awkward person," means lacking a natural facility with social cues, so that attending to and displaying them requires a conscious effort. "What awkward people need is guidance about how to navigate the social world with their unique perspective," for example, by reminding themselves to focus on social cues, look at eyes instead of ears, and so on.

On Tashiro's account, awkwardness is "dispositional," the result of attentional patterns "powered by neurological hardware that is as heritable as one's body weight or running speed" (2017: 23). If this is right, why not offer a dispositional analysis, identifying an awkward person as someone especially disposed either to experience awkwardness, end up in awkward situations, or elicit awkward feelings in others? One reason to be wary of conflating awkwardness with attention to social cues is that what causes awkward feelings in others and in oneself might be different: my failures to make eye contact might make you feel awkward, but not me. As we discussed above, using awkward as a description in this sense seems to mean, "someone who makes others feel awkward." I am also skeptical that there's a unified attentional deficit underlying the category of people we describe as awkward.[17] Some people may

---

[16] The terms "vertical" and "horizontal" refer to knowledge passed down from one generation to another versus between peers, respectively. So, very young children learn from their parents; as they get older, they're more likely to imitate peers (horizontal learning). For discussion see Gallois et al. 2018 and Garfield et al. 2016.

[17] Tahiro equates social awkwardness with what's known as the "broader autism phenotype," which refers to individuals who score outside the mean, but below clinical levels, on autism screening questionnaires. Less formally, it is also used to refer to individuals who exhibit some traits associated with autism, but don't meet the criteria for diagnosis. See Ruzich et al. 2016.

indeed require different sorts of social cues, or may need to make a more conscious effort to attend to social input, a point I discuss below. But even if we agree that what makes someone awkward is a lack of responsiveness to social cues, using "awkward" as a description obscures more than it illuminates, because there are any number of reasons why this might be.

Alternatively, awkwardness might be a component of a different personality trait, such as shyness (Crozier 1990: 3). Some individuals may be more prone to emotions that tend to be confused with awkwardness, such as shame and embarrassment; these individuals may even come to think of themselves as awkward (Miller 1995; Tangney et al. 2007). And people prone to shyness or social anxiety may label themselves "socially awkward" as a defense mechanism (Shepperd & Arkin 1990). So, we can understand the confusion here—why it might seem to people that they (or others) are awkward. But as we'll see later, self-conscious emotions and awkwardness are two different things.

Another reason for avoiding such descriptions involves concerns about how trait ascriptions of awkwardness are deployed, and against whom. Describing someone as awkward can be a way of signaling our disinclination to engage with them: we deploy the label "awkward" as a way to justify our unwillingness to interact with them or hear their claims. And as we'll see in chapter 5, awkwardness tends to arise in our interactions with certain groups or individuals for reasons that have nothing to do with character: for example, because of social norms and stigma surrounding disability, or our discomfort acknowledging class, race, or fatness.[18]

The account here might best be described as a "social model of awkwardness": rather than describing individuals as socially awkward, we should think of awkwardness as a social production.[19]

---

[18] On disability, see Madera & Henbl 2012; Hebl, Tickel, & Heatherton 2000.

[19] The term references the social model of disability, on which disability is understood not as a property of individuals, but as something arising from the interaction between individual and environment. For an overview and critique, see Terzi 2004. I return to this point in chapter 6.

A similar point has been made regarding our shifting understanding of neurodivergence. While one way of thinking about autism is that it involves a deficit in social understanding, another way is in terms of the interplay or misfit between autistic people and our social norms and spaces:

> Many autistics, for instance, find common social spaces such as bars or coffee shops to be difficult to manage given the sensory experiences they often encounter there. Or the need for increased processing time before responding can make participating in group discusses that switch topics quickly difficult . . . the real issue is a disconnect between the space and individuals' natural embodiment and mode of interaction. Rather than being a "problem" with one person, the issue is a disconnect between what is expected by those with the social privilege, here neurotypicals, and the modes of embodiment most comfortable for autistic individuals. (Timpe 2022: 172)

If some people seem more awkward than others, this is partly because of the sorts of situations they find themselves in, and partly because of the social cues they receive (or don't) from others. It's possible that some people are largely indifferent to social cues or concerns. These people (about whom I'll say more in the next section) aren't awkward, but they might be a kind of sociopath—awkwardness psychopaths, as it were. But the person who never seems to be able to make small talk, who always seems ill at ease, or makes others feel a little less at ease—that person isn't awkward. And if that person is you: you're not awkward, either.

1.10 Conclusion

I've analyzed awkwardness as the property that arises when we lack a social script to guide us through a situation or interaction.

As we've seen, there are a number of ways this can happen, because not only do scripts embed various types of information (from roles to behaviors to norms), they require us to coordinate our expectations and beliefs with others. So, my ability to identify and execute a script depends not just on what I know and can do, but on our willingness and ability to coordinate and share knowledge with others. In this sense, awkwardness is not just subjective but intersubjective. In the next chapter, I look more closely at the subjective experience of feeling awkward.

2
Feeling Awkward

2.1 Introduction: Awkward Feelings

In this chapter, I'll talk about feeling awkward: what is it like to experience awkwardness? How is it different from related feelings? Are some people more or less prone to feeling awkward than others? I'll explore how awkward feelings relate to emotions like shame and embarrassment. And I'll argue that feeling awkward isn't an emotion. While feeling awkward is causally connected to embarrassment, shame, and anxiety, it's not reducible to any of them.

A few more words about terminology: in the last chapter, I explained that "awkwardness" refers to a property that arises during social interactions. In section 1.9, I argued that things are awkward when they have the property of awkwardness; I also argued that people are not awkward and we shouldn't describe them as such. But what about the feelings that characterize awkward situations? Referring to these as "awkwardness" would confuse things here, because I'm saying that awkwardness is something that comes out of the interaction, not just a feeling. So, I use "feeling awkward" to describe the subjective experience that accompanies episodes of awkwardness—an experience characterized by uncertainty, self-consciousness, and discomfort. I also, at times, refer to these three states as "awkward feelings." That description isn't perfect, because there are feelings which themselves might be unscripted—feelings that operate outside our realm of social scripts, and challenge our ordinary social routines and practices.[1]

---

[1] I have in mind something similar to what Jaggar (1989) calls "outlaw emotions."

It's interesting to consider how and when emotions themselves might be awkward, but it's not the question I take up in this chapter.

Chapter 1 focused on where and why we encounter awkwardness in our everyday lives. This chapter focuses on the inner experience of feeling awkward: what is it like? What distinguishes it from other forms of discomfort and self-consciousness? I begin by discussing the possibility that some people might not experience awkward feelings, before turning to the question of how to characterize the state of feeling awkward. It's not an emotion, I argue, despite its similarities to the paradigmatically self-conscious emotions of guilt and shame. Because awkwardness is a shared production, the feeling of it isn't a reaction to our individual behavior (or another's). Instead, it's a reaction to insufficient social cues or information. It alerts us to a problem, but it doesn't offer us a solution. It shares some concerns and functions with anxiety, too, but there are important differences between the two. In distinguishing awkward feelings from these others, I also address the phenomenon of cringing, which I argue is not in fact a characteristic of awkwardness—when we describe things as "cringeworthy," we're actually talking about a different feeling altogether. And I explain why these distinctions matter: because awkwardness, embarrassment, shame, and anxiety all have different causes, pose different problems, and require different solutions.

2.2 The "Awkwardness Psychopaths"

I've argued against the idea that there are awkward people. But what about the reverse claim: are there people who don't feel awkward at all—who are somehow immune from it?

There's not much evidence on this one way or the other when it comes to awkwardness specifically, because most studies focus on embarrassment. But this evidence offers us a starting point—it looks as though some people may be immune to embarrassment, and the reasons why are suggestive. For example, patients with certain types of frontal lobe damage have trouble attributing embarrassment to others (Berthoz et al. 2002). Another measure involves the "awkward moments test," in which individuals are asked to identify embarrassing moments in film clips; autistic people show impaired abilities to recognize embarrassing situations (Heavey et al. 2000). One explanation for these results is that both recognizing and experiencing embarrassment requires a theory of mind (Miller 2014). This would also explain why patients with certain neurological injuries (e.g., damage to the medial prefrontal cortex) don't seem to experience embarrassment (Beer et al. 2003). Embarrassment also seems to be linked to empathy and identification, which explains how we're able to feel embarrassed for others: to the extent that we identify with the embarrassed other, we share in their embarrassment.[2]

But one might wonder whether there might be people who can recognize awkwardness yet remain untroubled by it—"awkwardness psychopaths," as it were, who could recognize the awkwardness of various situations, but not feel awkward as a result. Perhaps this simply describes a psychopath, full stop. This is Kotsko's interpretation of *Seinfeld*: "I will concede that there are frequent awkward moments, but... None of the main characters actually sit and stew in their awkwardness, and I'd propose that that's because they are all essentially sociopaths. They cause awkwardness in others but don't truly feel it themselves, because they lack any real investment in the social order" (2010: 23).

The question of empathy's involvement might be settled by looking at psychopaths, but there seems to be little research on whether they experience embarrassment, much less awkwardness. The work that does exist on psychopaths and self-conscious emotion is mixed and tends to focus on shame (Lanciano &

---

[2] Lickel, Shrader, & Spanovic 2007; see Beer & Keltner for a discussion of the psychology of vicarious embarrassment.

Curci 2021; Blair et al. 1995). There are also self-reports in online forums, and here a typical response is that psychopaths don't feel awkward themselves (though some report feeling embarrassed or humiliated; more on the difference below), but are able to recognize when others do. A characteristic comment explains, "I realised I'd made him feel awkward, but I didn't feel any of the awkwardness... we said our goodbyes and went on our way. As soon as he was out of earshot my fiancée goes: 'God. How awkward was that?!'" (Quora.com)

Kotsko's interpretation of *Seinfeld* characters as sociopaths highlights the link between feeling shared discomfort and an "investment" in the social world; it also reveals that understanding what's missing from the awkwardness psychopath might help us better understand the self-consciousness involved in awkwardness and how it relates to other forms of evaluative self-consciousness like embarrassment, shame, and pride.

The term "self-conscious" is sometimes used to imply an anxious, heightened self-awareness. That's the kind of self-consciousness we associate with awkwardness. But more fundamentally, self-consciousness involves an awareness of ourselves as seen through others' eyes. This doesn't imply caring about others: we might take up this viewpoint with cold calculation, trying to figure out how to best manipulate our image; we might be proud of ourselves for something we know others would not admire, or feel unmoved by an accomplishment we know others would admire.[3] Unless we are in fact psychopaths, though, most of us are somehow affected or moved by thoughts of how others see us. O'Brien explains "ordinary self-consciousness" as involving "our capacity to be poised to soak in, be pervious to, to absorb, the evaluations of others in way that alters, and colours, our consciousness of ourselves" (2020: 557). This capacity is a fundamental part of our social nature, a fact brought

---

[3] For a discussion of the relationship between pride and others' esteem, see Taylor 1985, especially chapter 1.

out when we consider what it would be to lack it: "there may be rare individuals who come to be the sole arbiters of their sense of their social value ... the only gaze with the power to diminish them is their own. Those individuals are likely to be peculiarly insured against, inured from, or to have unusual atypical capacities to discount, the responses of others" (562). When we picture such an individual, we're picturing someone who has in a literal sense stopped caring about others: the ability to feel awkwardness, shame, or embarrassment as a result of seeing oneself through others' eyes is part of what it is to invest others with significance.

That people vary in their proneness—or lack thereof—to awkwardness shows that our facility with social scripts and the extent to which we care about them can come apart. While feeling awkward involves heightened self-consciousness in the sense of thinking and caring about others' appraisals, one can make a situation awkward without so caring, by diverging from or muddying the social script. In other words, while feeling awkward requires a degree of investment in others' opinions, making things awkward doesn't. And insofar as some people are more attentive to social cues than others, some people will be more susceptible to feeling awkward. Indeed, as we'll see in chapters 3 and 5, this might mean that certain individuals or groups—those tasked with the emotional work of making others comfortable, for example—are particularly affected by, and susceptible to manipulation from, awkwardness. I'll come back to this in the next chapter, when I start to build my case for the normative significance of awkwardness. In the remainder of this chapter, I continue to examine its subjective aspects.

2.3 Awkward: The Feeling about Nothing?

In chapter 1, I claimed that feeling awkward doesn't tell us about other people, or the world around us, so much as respond to gaps in our own social knowledge and navigation. In this sense, awkward really is a feeling about nothing; it responds not to the presence of anything, but to the absence of a social script. That's not disqualifying per se—emotions can represent loss (for example, sadness) or absence (anxiety is arguably a response to the absence of a plan, a point I'll return to later), but the elicitors of awkward are too diffuse to present us with a unified content. Moreover, in the case of these other emotions, there's not only a characteristic elicitor but a characteristic content or intentionality to the subjective phenomenology. That's not the case here. In her book *Ugly Feelings*, Ngai describes the eponymous experiences as having "relatively weak intentionality," an "indistinctness if not absence of object." Like her "feelings," awkwardness is aptly described as "diagnostic rather than strategic . . . concerned with *inaction* in particular" (2005: 22).[4]

Feeling awkward does lend itself to certain kinds of behavior—or lack thereof. There's hesitation, stuttering, or just freezing; we withdraw eye contact. But any facial expression or behavior might express feeling awkward, depending on the circumstance. A smile, a gape, a grimace, a hand to the forehead—none of these is an uncommon gesture when one is feeling awkward. Moreover, feeling awkward often manifests in no behavior at all. Physical posture is no more helpful here: we might shift back and forth, or remain frozen to the spot. Nor does feeling awkward come with physiological changes. Contrast this with fear, anger, or disgust, which essentially involve bodily responses: the flush of anger, the rapid heart rate of fear, the nausea of genuine physical disgust. Awkwardness doesn't have a characteristic physiological response.

For all these reasons, I don't think feeling awkward is an emotion. Awkward feelings lack enough of the core features shared by most theories of emotion to disqualify them from counting as such. Specifically, awkward feeling lacks intentional content,

---

[4] See also Kotsko 2010, who discusses the possibility of understanding awkwardness as a feeling or mood.

characteristic physical displays, physiological changes, and action tendencies. My claim is not that any of these are necessary conditions for counting as an emotion, nor that the collection is sufficient—I don't want to defend a particular theory of emotion here. But given that feeling awkward doesn't require any of these features, we lack reason to classify it as an emotion.

Readers may object that I've overlooked a rather obvious component of awkwardness, namely, cringing. We describe situations as "cringeworthy," which suggests that they merit a cringing response.[5] This is an example of a "fittingness" approach to analyzing emotions, according to which a response or emotion is explained in terms of the conditions under which it would be appropriate to feel it. For example, sadness represents loss; sadness is fitting just in cases where a loss has been suffered. Anger represents an insult; being insulted is a condition under which it's fitting to feel angry.[6] With that in mind, why not analyze awkwardness as an emotion, cringing as the characteristic expression, and cringeworthiness as the property which makes feeling awkward a fitting response?

It might be tempting to go this route, but it would be a mistake. Contrary to popular belief, cringing isn't actually part of awkwardness, and it's not involved in feeling awkward. Instead, the association between cringing and awkwardness is retrospective, and comes from the fact that awkwardness gets confused with, and is causally linked to, two actually cringeworthy emotions: shame and embarrassment.

Cringing occurs when we experience embarrassment or shame, whether first- or second-hand, occurrent or retrospective. We think

---

[5] *Cringeworthy* is also the title of a 2018 book by Melissa Dahl, about the psychology of embarrassment and awkwardness, though it doesn't involve any of the views about fittingness described here.

[6] This is not the same as saying it's *good* to feel these things—fittingness is a dimension of appraisal that is normative but distinct from moral appraisal. It's more like appropriateness. For more on the distinction, see D'Arms & Jacobson 2000 on "the moralistic fallacy." The analyses of anger and sadness here are intended as examples of fittingness analyses; I don't mean to commit to them myself. For a defense of the claim about anger, see Nussbaum 2016.

of awkward moments as "cringeworthy" not because we cringe during them, but because we cringe when remembering our own awkward moments or witnessing others'. Remembering an awkward moment isn't itself awkward—it's shameful, or embarrassing. We often mistake what we feel when remembering awkward moments for what we felt during them. This is why we frequently mistake embarrassment for awkwardness, and vice versa: cringing accompanies our thoughts or memories of awkward, shameful, and embarrassing situations, and therefore becomes closely linked with these emotions, despite the fact that they're importantly distinct in other ways (which we'll examine below).

First, let's distinguish the feeling of cringing from the rise of "cringe" as a description. As it's used colloquially, "cringe" functions as a reaction to another's embarrassment or failure, rather than as an expression of awkwardness. Describing something as "cringe" expresses pity or contempt. When someone's performance or behavior (or social media post) is cringe, it's not coming across the way they think it is. Social media and reality television are "hotbeds for cringe... Here is a person standing up in public to say something that will be received in a way completely unlike what she had hoped or planned" (Tiffany 2022). But this use of "cringe"—which has, in recent months, been applied to everyone from Nancy Pelosi to Harry and Meghan to wearing Crocs, and might equally well apply to a philosopher attempting to offer an academic analysis of the term—is different from the sense that interests us here, which is the inner sensation of cringing.

Phenomenologically, the experience of cringing involves a self-deprecating withdrawal, a visceral curling in on oneself, a feeling in the pit of one's stomach that's not quite painful, but more than a knot. Cringing is more transient and weaker than self-loathing; harsher than laughing at oneself. We cringe when we're embarrassed and we cringe when we're ashamed. We don't cringe when we're feeling awkward. The mistaken association of cringing with awkwardness tells us two things: first, we're not great at disentangling our awkward experiences from our shameful or embarrassing ones, and second, much of the discomfort of awkward experiences remains when we observe or recollect them from a distance. Because we cringe both when feeling shame and when remembering our awkward moments, we can confuse an awkward memory for a shameful one, or mistake a topic that's awkward to discuss for one we're ashamed to broach. Likewise, cringing is a symptom of embarrassment, and we're often embarrassed by our own or others' awkward moments, so cringing and awkwardness do tend to correlate—but the mediating factor is either embarrassment or shame. Cringing isn't a direct result of awkwardness itself, but part of an experience which responds to awkwardness, among other things. This matters because as we'll see, shame indicates a normative attitude toward the behavior in question—so feeling shame at the memory of an awkward situation can lead us to conclude that awkwardness is somehow shameful and involves a normative transgression, rather than a lack of guidance. It can also confuse us into misattributing our shame to the awkward situation, thus mistakenly concluding that talking about periods, or sex, is shameful (rather than awkward). I return to this point in chapter 3, where I discuss how awkwardness creates confusion around social norms and accountability. In the second half of this chapter, I elaborate on the difference between awkward feelings and self-conscious emotions.

2.4 Self-Consciousness and Self-Conscious Emotions

We're self-conscious by nature. From a reflective philosophical perspective, this is a virtue; from a psychological view, it's a bit of a puzzle. For example, Fessler (2007: 178) wonders, why, given our limited cognitive capacity, do "humans expend so much of this important resource in both (1) monitoring the extent to which others conform to cultural standards, and (2) monitoring the extent to which our own behavior is being monitored?" The answer is that we're a cooperative species. Not only do we rely on one another; we rely on our ability to rely on one another. That means that others' compliance with group norms is my business, even if their actions don't involve me. Gossip plays a crucial role in forming and maintaining alliances, but also in reputation formation and management (Dunbar 2004). By gossiping about group members, we're able to share information about norm violations, and make better decisions about whom to ally ourselves with. Still, tracking reputation is only half the battle—a group where everyone has a shady reputation leaves us with no good options. What we need is a way not just to track people's reputations, but to make them care about their reputations. This is where the self-conscious emotions (SCEs) come in.

Self-conscious emotions "fundamentally involve people's reactions to their own characteristics or behavior" (Tangney 1996: 446). Some SCEs are positive—in addition to embarrassment, guilt, and shame, there's pride—but I focus mainly on the negative ones here. What unites SCEs is an essentially self-evaluative orientation: they're based on, and directed at, a certain representation of our own behaviors, characteristics, or self. SCEs benefit the agent by providing feedback about how well his behaviors meet others' relevant normative standards. (I'll say more about how this works in a moment.) But they also serve an important third-party function: displaying an SCE signals awareness of our normative shortcomings.[7] SCEs help us regulate the way we present ourselves to others, and they're useful for communicating awareness of, and remorse for, norm violations and social transgressions. In doing so, they serve two purposes: recognition and repair. They let others

---

[7] And perhaps our accomplishments. I don't discuss pride here, though arguably pride has a signaling function too, and a characteristic display. For signaling purposes, we can think of pride as telling others not that we've accomplished something, but that we take the accomplishment to be valuable. See Taylor 1985.

know that even though we've violated a norm, we still care about living up to social expectations and standards, thereby restoring group cohesion.[8] While alienating in the moment, SCEs like embarrassment and shame ultimately reintegrate individuals into the group. The withdrawal and submissive physical postures characteristic of guilt, shame, and embarrassment tell others we know we've transgressed; the aversiveness of the emotion motivates us to repair the norm violation and refrain from future transgressions. Experiencing and displaying SCEs is evidence of our sensitivity to shared group norms.

Self-conscious emotions may be particularly useful in contexts where the norm in question is not amenable to "official" sanctioning through punishment or reward. You can't get away with murder by blushing. But punishment is costly, so an emotion like embarrassment is a useful way to deal with milder transgressions, especially social gaffes or missteps—for example, when I accidentally interrupt a colleague during an important meeting, or clap during a pause in the concert. In these cases, punishing me is both too costly and too severe; we need a noninstitutional alternative, something that sanctions people without imposing the costs of punishment on others. The self-conscious emotions offer a solution.

2.5 Embarrassment

What's needed is some way to demonstrate my awareness I've screwed up; that I find that awareness uncomfortable; that I'm unlikely to do it again. Embarrassment is particularly well suited for this function, because it not only feels bad from a first-person perspective, it signals contrition. Embarrassment does this via its signature facial display, the blush: a hard-to-fake signal of contrition

---

[8] For argument to this effect, see Keltner & Buswell 1997; Thomas, DiScioli, & Pinker 2018.

that serves as a kind of appeasement. Blushing is also felt from the inside—we know when we're doing it—so it makes our embarrassment common knowledge (Thomas et al. 2018: 188). This explains why we respond more positively to norm violators who display embarrassment than to those who don't (Miller & Tangney 1994: 275)—blushing is a genuine sign of contrition, because we can't blush on command; we can't fake it.

Given my argument against classifying feeling awkward as an emotion, one might wonder whether it should instead be considered a type of embarrassment. For example, Keltner and Anderson (2000) list awkward as a "component feeling" of embarrassment, and Crozier (1990: 2) talks about various "tokens" of embarrassment—synonyms one finds in everyday language, such as "humiliation, mortification." Might awkwardness be one of these? Parrott (2004: 137) notes, "The word embarrassment is applied to a range of reactions," one of which includes "social awkwardness rooted in difficulty acting in specific situations." And Miller (1996: 14–15) describes "sensations of foolish awkwardness" as characteristic of embarrassment. On Miller's view, awkward interactions are a subtype of embarrassment, distinguished by the fact that two people are involved in producing it (1996: 62–64). This is striking, since it seems to mark a significant difference between awkwardness and other types of embarrassment, but Miller does not seem troubled by the discrepancy. Awkward behavior has also been identified as a manifestation of both shyness and embarrassment (Buss & Briggs 1984; Cheek & Briggs 1990; Crozier 1990; Harré 1990), so why not simply classify awkwardness as a token of one (or both) of these?

This is a reasonable question. In one sense, it might seem like not much turns on the difference, and many of the arguments in the following chapters are independent of the taxonomy offered here. But I think it's important to recognize awkwardness as a phenomenon with a distinct set of causes and explanations, because if we don't, we'll fail to recognize opportunities for remedy and change. Recall our earlier observation about the conflation of awkwardness and shame: if we don't recognize awkward feelings as having a distinct cause, we risk making a mistaken normative assessment of the situation, viewing it as involving a wrong rather than a lack of guidance. I'll say more about this at the end of chapter 5 when I discuss shame and taboos, but for now, note that distinguishing awkward feelings from embarrassment allows us to distinguish social transgressions from social dislocation—and that, in turn, allows us to locate the correct remedy, which is creating new social scripts, not repairing rifts in our relationships. But a second reason for recognizing awkward feelings as distinct from embarrassment is that it makes for a clearer picture of embarrassment itself, an emotion that turns out to be surprisingly complicated to analyze.

In the remainder of this section, I'll outline several alternative theories of embarrassment. As we'll see, psychologists and philosophers have struggled to pin down its nature and causes. I'll argue that once we distinguish embarrassment and awkwardness, things become a bit clearer: awkwardness is able to explain a category of phenomena that theories of embarrassment struggle with, and the pared-down category of the embarrassing becomes a bit more manageable.

Embarrassment has been described as providing "coherence amidst psychic chaos" (Keltner & Anderson 2000: 188). Yet looking at the literature on embarrassment itself, we find more chaos than coherence. Not only accounts, but taxonomies of those accounts proliferate: Sabini and Silver argue that there are three main theories of embarrassment; Keltner and Buswell identify five. For our purposes, we can divide up the content and causes of embarrassment, as posited in these theories, into three main camps: "dramaturgical theories," "social faux pas" theories, and "sticky situation" theories. I will argue that embarrassment is explained by faux pas theories, and that the remaining two theories—dramaturgical theories and sticky situation theories—pick out shame and feeling awkward. Once we carve up the space this way, not only do we better understand the difference between awkwardness and embarrassment, but the category of the embarrassing becomes more manageable and unified. I'll start by reviewing the features of embarrassment, before looking at each view in turn and making my case for embarrassment as response to social faux pas.

The basic sensation of embarrassment involves wishing to hide; a desire to escape the situation, a shrinking from others' gaze; feeling foolish; being highly aware of others' attention and judgment. The urge to shrink inward is accompanied by the submissive postures and displays described above: Keltner and Buswell (1997: 264) catalog "self-abasement... feelings of inadequacy... head movements down, face covering, and postural shrinkage." (If that sounds like cringing: yes.) Embarrassment has some positive aspects, including "affiliative" feelings such as "amusement... the pronounced inclination to laugh... smiles, lip wipes, and puckers."

According to dramaturgical theories, embarrassment occurs when our social performance fails and leaves us exposed, either because something threatens the identity we're claiming for ourselves (the smooth, competent professional suddenly realizes his fly is open), or because there's too much attention on us, leaving us flustered (this explains how we can be embarrassed by good things, like praise). For example, Miller and Tangney (1994) write that embarrassment occurs "whenever unwanted events threaten the social images people wish to maintain." Sabini and Silver (1997: 11) complicate matters further by distinguishing cases where "a flaw in the actor's character" is revealed, which bring about shame, from cases where "a flaw in the character being enacted" is revealed, which bring about embarrassment. This brings out the fact that dramaturgical theories allow for significant overlap between shame and embarrassment, which ought to give us pause: when we ask what kinds of events cause us to lose face, or what kinds of events reveal a flaw in character or performance, the answer might be that the event reveals something about us, or that it reveals a social ineptitude. In the former case, we have shame, about which I say more in the next section; in the latter case, we have embarrassment, but embarrassment stemming from a social gaffe or faux pas. In other words, faux pas theories of embarrassment have the advantage not only of fitting with the functional profile of embarrassment, but of explaining the "failed performance" intuition by giving an account of the failure itself.

There's another variation of the dramaturgical view that needs addressing: the idea that embarrassment is caused by exposure. This is expressed more clearly by philosophers than psychologists. For example, Taylor (1985) argues that embarrassment is the result of feeling exposed in a discrediting way, either by oneself or someone one associates with. And Purshouse (2001: 530) analyzes embarrassment as "essentially about the exposure of one person to another," where exposure means that "an aspect of one person ... enters the experience or thoughts of another." Embarrassment can result for the exposed, the "exposee," or both, but the experience must be aversive—this is (according to Purshouse) what distinguishes a welcome declaration of love from an embarrassing one. But what makes the exposure aversive, and why does attention lead to embarrassment? The question shows how dramaturgical theory conflates two problems that can arise in our performances of self. On the one hand, we have the problem of the discredited self, which causes a loss of face, which in turn causes embarrassment or shame (about which more below). Embarrassment also offers a remedy: when I do something discrediting, the repair-oriented displays of embarrassment enact humility, letting others know I'm aware of my failings and I feel bad about them. On the other hand, we have the problem of conflicting selves, or uncertainty about which self to bring to the table. This is an awkward problem.

Taylor suggests that the real discrediting is done not by the exposure of some embarrassing feature of the self, but by the exposee's flustered response. Giving the example of a party where a guest suddenly begins to pray, embarrassing the other guests, Taylor notes, "Nor would that guest feel embarrassed who knew exactly what to do... The guest who is embarrassed neither remains uninvolved nor knows what to do. He thinks he ought to do something, but cannot think what, or dithers between possible alternatives" (1985: 71).[9] What exposes the guest is not a discrediting action or feature per se, but the discrediting performance of not knowing what to do in response. Embarrassment is "a social emotion," involving a "tension between the felt demand and the inability to respond." This combination of the social demand to act and the inability to respond distinguishes the dramaturgical view from the social faux pas view. But it also reveals that the dramaturgical view performs better as a theory of awkwardness than of embarrassment.

Suppose we take cases like Taylor's and classify them as instances of awkwardness rather than embarrassment. Left with performances that fail due to faux pas or gaffes, the dramaturgical view comes to resemble the "social faux pas" view of embarrassment. As the name suggests, on this view, embarrassment is caused by social gaffes or faux pas: social norm violations or failures to follow certain social conventions (e.g., Silver et al. 1987).[10]

A faux-pas theory of embarrassment makes sense of many features, and fits well with the functional analysis offered above. On this view, embarrassment is a response to relatively benign social norm violations. I've already explained how this works functionally, so I won't belabor the point here. And once we distinguish social faux pas from dramaturgical exposures and sticky situations, the set of cases embarrassment is tasked with explaining becomes a lot more manageable. Benziman begins his conceptual analysis of embarrassment by acknowledging that "finding the common feature to various ordinary cases is harder than might seem at first."

---

[9] Thanks to John Lawless for pointing out the connection to this example.
[10] I am simplifying the distinctions here somewhat to avoid overburdening the reader with taxonomy; as noted above, the tripartite division used here is just one of several found in the psychology literature. For example, Miller (1996, 2014) combines aspects of the social evaluation theory with faux pas and argues that embarrassment is caused by a public failure to meet normative expectations; this view falls somewhere between dramaturgic theories and faux-pas theories.

He then sets out to do just that, with a list of examples ranging from a groom walking down the aisle with a tomato-juice stain on his white tuxedo to[11] "meet[ing] your ex-partner for the first time after you have broken up. Both of you find the situation embarrassing" and "meet[ing] a colleague of yours for the first time after his wife was killed . . . you are not sure what to say . . . both of you find the situation embarrassing" (2019: 78). Ultimately, what these cases have in common is that "we are not well equipped to deal with the situation. We are not at ease . . . we do not know what to do about it" (84). But what explains the first case is the faux pas of wearing a stained shirt; the second and third are cases where we don't know how to act. In other words, the first case is embarrassing; the second two are awkward. Awkward feelings arise when we don't know how to act; embarrassment arises when we act in ways we know we're not supposed to. Embarrassment happens when we lose face because of a gaffe; awkwardness happens when we lose face because we couldn't decide which face to "wear" or "perform," or we failed to coordinate our "selves."

One objection might be that gaffes sometimes become awkward, which suggests that awkwardness is actually a symptom of embarrassment. But in fact, awkwardness results from gaffes that lead to sticky situations: situations where we don't know how to make the necessary social repairs. Sometimes this is because it's public and we don't know whether other people expect—or want—an acknowledgment. If we view embarrassment through a functional lens, it makes sense that it would come into play most readily when the gaffe happens in front of people we interact with regularly, and less readily on one-shot interactions. That's because we have more invested in repairing relationships; when interacting with someone we'll never see again, the reputational stakes are lower, and we also feel less confident making assumptions about their expectations.

---

[11] As Benziman notes, the example is originally discussed in Sabini & Silver 1997.

Another possibility is that the situation becomes awkward because to acknowledge the gaffe would put someone else in an uncomfortable situation. This brings us to the "sticky situation" theory of embarrassment, which I'm claiming is actually better understood as a theory of awkwardness. Recall our hypothetical example with which we began the book, of a graduate student having dinner with a distinguished speaker when food flies out of her mouth and lands on the speaker's sweater. One option is to openly acknowledge the incident and apologize. But doing so implicates them, too—it acknowledges the stain on them. So perhaps it would be better for them to simply pretend it never happened. Or maybe they don't know it happened, in which case we would be better off just ignoring the incident—but we can't be sure. This uncertainty is where awkwardness comes in.

If embarrassment is a reparative response, then transforming awkward moments into embarrassing ones can be an improvement—provided it happens relatively quickly, we can assimilate the uncertain and unscripted situation to a more familiar one. As Miller (2014: 132) notes, "embarrassed people are more likely to try to maintain and repair their current interactions than they are to run and hide," and therefore, "embarrassment usually has a constructive effect on its social situations." Awkwardness has no such appeasement function, no corresponding display. Because embarrassment follows and repairs social norm violations, it's a scripted display of emotion: it gives us a way to feel, and a way to display that feeling to others. When someone displays embarrassment, it allows us to reassure them and put things at ease. Note how blushing elicits beneficence: we tell people, "Don't be embarrassed"; we recount our own embarrassing stories; we try to change the subject or create a distraction, allowing the embarrassed person a chance to regain composure. By manifesting contrition, embarrassment earns our forgiveness and goodwill.[12]

---

[12] See Keltner & Buswell 1997; Keltner & Anderson 2000 for discussion of this point.

Readers might be suspicious of this benign picture, since embarrassment can be painful—even cruel. Billig (2001) critiques "nice guy" theories of embarrassment that omit the pleasure we sometimes take in ridiculing others, and it's true that embarrassment has a dark side: humiliation. Miller (1993: 148–149) describes humiliation's punitive aspect, which takes aim at our pretensions and vanity. It deflates aspirations to status or coolness: "Humiliation is firm, embarrassment is light. Humiliation is rough justice, embarrassment a gentle slap on the wrist. Embarrassment is a close relative of amusement. . . . But one senses that if humiliation has anything to do with amusement, that amusement would be dark indeed." The pain of humiliation (because it is, as the foregoing description indicates, painful) haunts us for years, unlike the relatively fleeting sensation of embarrassment. Embarrassing stories are recounted over drinks; humiliating stories are recounted at therapy, if at all.

2.6 Shame

Shame is slightly easier to distinguish from awkwardness than embarrassment, though harder to eradicate. I say "slightly" because shame shares certain phenomenological features with embarrassment: both involve the sensation of shrinking, wishing one could disappear; both are linked to appeasement, their displays playing a reparative role.[13] It's more enduring than either awkwardness or embarrassment; we often feel shame about events that happened days, weeks, months, or years in the past. Awkward moments are one source of shame, though people were significantly less likely to cite "awkward" as a description of a time when they experienced shame than when they experienced embarrassment (27% vs. 73%,

---

[13] See Keltner & Buswell 1997; Keltner & Anderson 2000; Sabini & Silver 1997.

respectively; Miller & Tangney 1994: 280). But the link between shame and awkwardness goes deeper than this.

Like embarrassment, shame is a self-conscious emotion, involving displays of contrition and appeasement. The differences lie in the scope of the evaluation involved: while embarrassment responds to individual social gaffes, shame attaches to the whole person (Tangney 1995, 116–117). So, one reason memories of awkward moments elicit shame is that they seem to reveal something about who we are. These are the memories that elicit retrospective, even visceral cringing; keep us up at night; make us want to hide even when we're alone. When we remember moments when we were awkward—when we didn't know the script—we sometimes feel ashamed, because we view them as failures, moments when we fell short in our performances as people. But as I'll argue throughout the book, these are collective failures, not individual ones, and it's important to recognize the difference. If shame is a response to personal failures,[14] then awkwardness is nothing to be ashamed of. Moreover, the two issues point us in different directions. Shameful failures point us inward, and the work to be done as a result of those failures is work on ourselves: we should become better people; we should live up to our values or our cultures' values.[15] Awkward moments point to a different remedy: we should look outward, at the kind of social scripts available to us, and ask how these are written and disseminated.

The causal relationship between shame and awkwardness is complicated by the fact that shame is one reason why topics or interactions become awkward in the first place. Shame around certain topics—like sex, or addiction—makes us shy away from

---

[14] This view is fairly common, but for discussion of the type of failure involved, see Calhoun 2004, Maibom 2010, and Thomason 2015. The discussion here has focused on psychological theories of shame; I say more about philosophical theories at the end of chapter 5.

[15] As noted below, there's some disagreement over whether the standards involved in shame are the agents' own, or those of her group. See Calhoun 2004 and Maibom 2010 for discussion.

discussing them. This in turn prevents us from acquiring social scripts with which to navigate them. We'll discuss the implications of this in more detail when we get to chapters 5 and 6, but for now I want to just note one consequence of the relationship: shame makes a topic awkward, and awkwardness can make us ashamed. This helps explain why we sometimes feel ashamed for violating standards we don't actually endorse: emotions like shame and embarrassment involve a commitment, not to a particular norm per se, but to the shared set of standards operative in our social environment.[16] When we feel ashamed of doing something we don't think is wrong, we're not ashamed of the behavior per se, but of failing to conform to group norms (I say more about this aspect of shame at the end of chapter 5).

I'll continue to explore this point about conformity to norms in the next chapter. In the last and final section of this chapter, I turn my attention to the other two elements of awkward feeling: discomfort and uncertainty. I discuss these in the context of awkward feelings, as well as the related but distinct experience of anxiety. On paper, feeling uncertain, self-conscious, and uncomfortable seems to describe both anxiety and awkwardness, but as we'll see, there are significant differences between the two.

2.7 Awkward, Uncomfortable, Anxious

In chapter 1, I briefly surveyed the elements of awkward feeling: discomfort, uncertainty, and self-consciousness. Here, I want to say more about these, starting with discomfort. Discomfort is especially tricky to pin down; it can be hard to identify its cause and direction. For some philosophers, this gives us an extra reason to be wary of it.

---

[16] See Calhoun 2004 for argument to this effect, which I discuss further in section 5.8.

Munch-Jurisic (2020: 244) argues that discomfort is best understood as a kind of "rudimentary affect" that can "push us in many different directions." Since discomfort lacks a clear intentionality, we can attribute it to a variety of factors: others who might be present at the time; a belief or thought about ourself and our behavior; our uncertainty; or the awareness that we have certain conflicting attitudes, goals, or beliefs. This ambiguity means that discomfort lends itself to abuse—bias can lead us to pin our discomfort on the presence of those who didn't laugh at the inappropriate joke, rather than the joke-teller himself. The point could be made equally well in terms of awkwardness: because it's not always clear whose behavior is the cause of an awkward situation, our identification of the cause may track and amplify existing biases. (In chapter 5, I discuss this point as it applies to social scripts about gender and emotional comfort.) But feeling awkward is not reducible to discomfort: one can be uncomfortable for various reasons, including frustration or annoyance.

Discomfort can manifest physically and/or affectively. In the case of feeling awkward, it's accompanied by an intense self-awareness and uncertainty, which can manifest in feelings of being frozen, while also being highly aware of one's body and speech. The awkward situation becomes highly salient: it feels like everyone's attention is focused on it, and time seems to slow down (Clegg 2012a, 2012b). In this respect, discomfort resembles another form of affect: anxiety.[17] Indeed, anxiety and feeling awkward have an overlapping phenomenological profile—like feeling awkward, anxiety involves discomfort, self-consciousness, and uncertainty. As with awkwardness, it's this uncertainty that can make anxiety useful: it draws attention to areas where social resources are lacking (a point I discuss in more detail in chapter 3).

---

[17] I use the term "affect" here, but Kurth argues that anxiety is an emotion, though his theory of emotion is significantly more complex than anything I've discussed here; see his 2018, chapter 2, on anxiety and the biocognitive model of emotion.

One way anxiety and awkwardness relate is via "social anxiety": anxiety about the prospect of awkwardness. We anticipate it; we dread it; we do what we can to avoid it. As Kurth (2018) points out, one of the main sources of social anxiety is the idea that we might not correctly identify the social norms in play, a consequence of which would be awkwardness. So, it's not a stretch to say that much of our social anxiety is directed at the prospect of awkwardness. Kurth goes on to argue that anxiety plays a valuable moral and epistemic role, drawing our attention to potential challenges and conflicts, particularly in the moral domain. I've claimed that awkwardness plays a valuable epistemic role by highlighting gaps and conflicts in our social scripts. Given the overlap in these functions, it's not surprising that there are similarities between anxiety and awkwardness: both are responses to uncertainty; both are aversive. But there are significant differences, too.

Anxiety is prospective: it anticipates "threats and challenges that are unpredictable, uncontrollable, and uncertain in nature" (Kurth 2018: 33). Awkwardness is occurrent: when we feel awkward, it's because the awkwardness is happening right now. Anxiety prompts us to assess and minimize risk in future scenarios, whereas awkwardness is concerned with what's already happening. Often, what we're anxious about is the (future) possibility of experiencing awkwardness, or of committing the sorts of transgressions that cause awkwardness. In this sense, the two may be closely linked, even causally related. But anxiety is not confined to the social realm: one can feel anxious alone, or anxious about things that happen when one is alone—or even anxious about being alone.

These are significant differences, and they give us reason to resist any identification of awkwardness and anxiety. But the two might still play similar roles in our moral deliberations, even if they enter the process at different points. Kelly (2021: 254) suggests that anxiety might facilitate norm creation by heightening our awareness of "normative ambiguity or conflict," interrupting "the intuitive and relatively unthinking kind of cognition that often drives behavior guided by internalized norms." This interruption in our smooth, intuitive, frictionless social navigation is not unlike awkwardness. But anxiety's prospective nature means that it creates possibilities for rumination and a deliberate approach to normative lacunae; awkwardness's spontaneous onset forces us to improvise.

2.8 Awkwardness as Misattunement

Throughout this chapter, I've said a lot about what awkward feelings are not: they're not an emotion, not embarrassment or shame, not anxiety. What distinguishes the discomfort that characterizes awkwardness, and why do we find it aversive? One option is to simply accept Munch-Jurisic's characterization of discomfort as affectively basic, but I think there is more we can say about the phenomenology of feeling awkward, and a good place to start is by thinking about the social nature of awkwardness. The feelings that accompany awkwardness reflect its source in a lack of social guidance. To see how, it will help to look at a very different kind of experience: attunement.

Haybron describes attunement in terms of safety and familiarity, which enable confidence: "When an organism is in familiar and safe circumstances, where it has mastery of its environment, it can let down its defenses... and confidently engage in whatever pursuits it wishes. The Stoics might have said that the individual in that situation finds her life *oikeion*—familiar—to her" (2008: 116–117). This is a useful contrast with the picture of awkwardness I've been painting, since it helps us see what we're lacking when we experience awkwardness: a certain sense of "continuity or fit between self and world." Attunement also involves "somatic confidence," the state of "feeling wholly at home in one's body." Haybron suggests that this experience is a fundamental aspect of human well-being (111–112). Reflecting on the concept of attunement helps us see why and how the experience of awkwardness is detrimental. The psychological elements of attunement—somatic confidence, the sense of familiarity and surety, the feeling of being at home in one's body and environment—are noticeably absent from awkward situations.

This also shows how physical awkwardness—not knowing how or where to move one's body, to stand, and so on—can create the psychic feelings characteristic of awkwardness. Indeed, Haybron uses the description "Nixonian awkwardness" to characterize the negative pole of physical attunement. To be physically misattuned is to experience many of these same feelings of alienation and insecurity; just as our emotional well-being and our physical well-being are linked, so are our emotional attunement and our physical attunement. I've avoided using the term "socially awkward," because it implies a contrasting category of "physically awkward"—and while we intuitively distinguish the two, doing so risks obscuring the extent to which social appraisals depend on physical performance. Our physical and social environments overlap, and misattunement in one is likely to manifest as misattunement with the other. Ahmed's (2014: 20) description of attunement as, "intercorporeal experience" captures the idea of (mis)attunement as a relationship between socially situated bodies, or bodies and their environment. Our attunement—or lack thereof—manifests in mundane, everyday activities like walking down the street, cases where we can find ourselves in or out of sync with surrounding bodies. And a lack of attunement, whether our own or others', is experienced as problematic.

The concept of attunement—more specifically, its failures—nicely captures the way in which mismatch or misfit between the individual and her environment, both physical and social, creates awkwardness. It also helps us see why the disvalue in awkwardness amounts to more than passing annoyance or discomfort. Even if the experience of awkward feelings is relatively short-lived, its implications for our well-being, our sense of security and confidence, and our relationships with others may not be. Disruptions in attunement are bad for us in any number of ways: we can end up scapegoating others for them; they disrupt group cohesion; perhaps most fundamentally, they feel bad. Attunement highlights the extent to which our well-being depends on group membership and the opinions of others. Ostracism and exclusion are painful, even in cases where we don't endorse the group's normative commitments.

2.9 Conclusion

I ended the last chapter by arguing that it's a mistake to label individuals "awkward"; the concepts of attunement and misattunement further illuminate why and how awkwardness is a social property rather than an individual one. The phenomenology of awkward feelings is likewise oriented toward the feeling of being out of sync with one's surroundings. In the next chapter, I explain why this matters and what it tells us. Why does awkwardness present as threatening, something to avoid? And why do we find it entertaining in certain contexts? The answer has to do with awkwardness's relationship to social norms and the epistemic resources these depend on—how our knowledge of social norms is maintained and revealed to others. In the next chapter, I explore the relationship between awkwardness and norms in more detail, beginning with a detour into the aesthetics of awkwardness.

3
Awkward, Socially

3.1 Introduction: From Aesthetics to Ethics?

Understanding our reactions to awkwardness, and the discrepancy between our reaction to observing it at a distance and up close and personal, helps us understand what's socially disruptive about it. I'll start by discussing the aesthetics of awkwardness, including the appeal (and aversiveness) of "cringe comedy." I'll go on to explain how awkwardness is linked to identity: fluency with social norms and scripts marks one as belonging, and awkwardness can mark one as an outsider. Specifically, I'll argue that awkwardness draws our attention to threats to social norms by indicating either that someone is an unreliable cooperator or that the status of a norm is itself uncertain. This will serve as the starting point for a discussion of how awkwardness relates to social norms, highlighting areas where they're unclear, and closing off opportunities to improve them.

The structure of this chapter is itself a little awkward, as it attempts to bridge two seemingly disparate topics. So, in section 3.2, I talk about the aesthetics of awkwardness with a focus on awkward comedy; in sections 3.3–3.5 I move to the relationship between awkwardness and social norms. These aren't unrelated: understanding the draw—and aversiveness—of observing awkwardness helps us understand why it's socially threatening. Our social norms, and the accountability they underwrite, depend on others' commitment; awkwardness shows that commitment to be shaky or unreliable. To understand how and why, we'll start with a closer look at our reactions to awkwardness.

3.2 The Aesthetics of Awkwardness

3.2.1 Awkward Comedy, Social Horror

I spent most of chapter 2 discussing the various ways in which experiencing awkwardness makes for an unpleasant experience, detailing the negative aspects of awkward feelings. This leaves us with a puzzle: why do we find watching awkwardness, in the form of awkward or "cringe" comedy, entertaining? This is an instance of a more general puzzle, wherein we seek out fictional representations of experiences or emotions that, in real life, we would find strongly aversive.[1] Paradoxically, the aversion is part of the appeal: awkwardness is an example of the "distancing-embracing" model of negative emotions (Meningaus et al. 2017). It draws us in and elicits a reaction, but we're able to enjoy it in a way we couldn't if it were actually happening to us, because we're witnessing it at a safe distance.

This brings out an interesting difference between awkward comedy and other paradoxically hedonic negative emotions, where we actually experience the negative emotion—for example, fear or disgust. In chapter 2, I argued that we don't cringe when we're *in* an awkward situation, but that cringing is a reaction we have from outside, when we observe or recollect awkwardness. One explanation of our emotional reaction to awkward comedy is that we're projecting ourselves into the social situation and feeling imagined, vicarious awkwardness. Another is that while watching awkwardness on screen, or reading about others' awkward interactions, we often feel second-hand embarrassment or even shame. The feeling of wanting to hide one's eyes, being unable to look at the screen—that's cringing, caused by observing someone else's awkwardness.[2]

---

[1] The observation that there's something paradoxical about this reaction is usually credited to Hume, in "Of Tragedy," though the observation that tragedy brings us pleasure goes back at least as far as Aristotle, who discusses it in the *Poetics*.

[2] My focus is on awkwardness in TV or movies, but arguably, it's present in books, too—my extremely unscientific sampling of friends and colleagues suggested sources

Compare this to watching a graphic sex scene with one's parents—that's awkward. So, the term "awkward comedy" is somewhat of a misnomer; the alternative term "cringe comedy" might be more accurate. Nonetheless, I'll use "awkward comedy" here, because the relevant feature is that we're watching awkwardness unfold.

Horror films, spicy foods, and gross-out humor are all instances of benign masochism—cases where we expose ourselves to safe doses of pain or danger, for the pleasure of experiencing both the sensation and its relief. To this list we can add awkward comedy: here, we expose ourselves to the sensation of social rejection or alienation through our identification with the awkward protagonist. Much as a roller coaster ride offers controlled access to the sensation of free-falling, a horror movie offers us access to feelings of suspense, terror, revulsion, and so on, without exposing ourselves to actual serial killers, ghosts, and so on.[3] Awkward comedy allows us to vicariously experience the fear of self-consciousness, social rejection, ostracism, and anxiety without actually placing ourselves in social danger. But as we noted above, our enjoyment of horror films presents a puzzle: why do we seek out films that give rise to fear and disgust? Likewise, why do we enjoy comedies that make us want to disappear behind the couch with second-hand cringing?

It's unsurprising that comedy and awkwardness overlap, since both essentially involve social disruption. As Berlant and Ngai (2017: 234) observe, "One worry comedy engages is formal or technical in a way that leads to the social: the problem of figuring out distinctions between things, including people, whose relation is mutually disruptive of definition. Classic comedy theory points to rapid frame breaking . . . as central to comedic pleasure."

---

ranging from Henry James (*The Ambassadors*) to *Harry Potter* (the scene where Harry goes on a date with Cho Chang).

[3] This suggests that the paradox as stated here is too simple: the answer is not to resolve a supposed tension between pleasure and pain, but to broaden our understanding of which states have hedonic value beyond just "pleasurable" ones. See Smuts 2009.

Comedy can also involve acknowledgment of an existing disruption or failure, thereby relieving the pressure of suppressing it. For example, Berlant (2017: 312) gives an extended analysis of "the combover genre" of comedy in terms of "the public pleasure that takes place when what had been an awkward open secret becomes explicit and available for pitiless mirth." But not all mirth is pitiless, and we often feel an unpleasant degree of empathy watching awkward situations unfold, even in fictional scenarios. This brings us back to the paradox: how are we able to feel the kind of vicarious cringe on which awkward comedy relies, and why do we enjoy it when we do?[4]

Both horror and comedy rely on incongruity: "the transgression of a category, a concept, a norm, or a commonplace expectation" (Carroll 1999: 154). In a way, this isn't a bad characterization of awkwardness itself, which involves the failure of an interaction to proceed according to expectations: like the jump scares produced by a monster's sudden appearance, the sudden failure of a script produces a reaction, even when we're observing from a safe distance (and even when we know it's inevitable). Awkward comedy is thus a kind of social horror.[5]

Kotsko (2010) spends most of his analysis of awkwardness on a detailed analysis of awkward comedies, including *The Office* (both UK and US versions) and the films of Judd Apatow. In awkward comedy, safety comes both from distance and identification. It's not just the relief of knowing the awkwardness isn't happening to us, but the double relief of seeing it happen to someone else. The horror of awkwardness is partly the feeling of isolation, of feeling like we're uniquely marked out and alienated by our social

---

[4] See Gaut 1993 for an overview of the paradox, and some solutions to it. Here, I focus on Carroll's 1999 proposal that the explanation lies in our reaction to a kind of boundary violation. See Levinson 2013 for a survey of perspectives on the issue and Strohl 2012 for a discussion of the paradox applied to horror.

[5] In fact, a prominent moral psychologist divulged, after hearing that I was writing a book about awkwardness, that he and his family told "awkward stories" around the campfire instead of the usual ghost or horror stories.

ineptitude. The promise of awkward comedy is that we're not. We can read this either as benign reassurance, or a more malign type of schadenfreude.

Laughter's role in defusing awkwardness is telling: when we laugh with someone, we're coordinating our affective display. This can be more or less sincere—awkward laughter isn't a full-throated belly laugh; it's more like an attempt to break a silence. But when laughter is sincere, it not only signals coordination, it also takes over—genuine laughter disrupts our physical composure, temporarily taking control of our behavior.[6] Ironically, by disrupting the disruption that is awkwardness, laughter gets us back on track.

3.2.2 Awkwardness and the Aesthetics of Action

Social norms are identity markers.[7] The way we worship, what foods we eat, and how we dress signal group membership. Etiquette does this, too, allowing for more fine-grained distinctions: not just which cultural group one belongs to, but which stratum of that group one occupies. When we observe someone in an awkward situation, we evaluate them as an outsider, someone who doesn't know the rules or norms, or who knows them superficially but hasn't internalized them. This might not always elicit dislike: the so-called pratfall effect refers to the idea that a person's errors can make them appear more likable; recently, this has inspired designers of robots to experiment with programming in hesitance and error to see if that makes the robots more "likable" and less uncanny. Like the evidence for the pratfall effect itself, the results have been mixed.[8]

---

[6] See Olin 2022 on the physical and psychological effects of mirth.
[7] See Kelly 2013, chapter 4, on "tribal instincts." Dunbar (2004) argues that dialect is also an in-group marker, signaling trustworthy cooperators.
[8] Aronson et al. 1966 introduce the idea of the pratfall effect; Weaver et al. 2002 discuss some failed attempts at replication. Regarding robots, see Mirnig et al. 2017 and Packard et al. 2019.

I've argued against the idea that there are awkward people—awkwardness is a property of situations, not a character trait. But we do react negatively to what we perceive as people's awkwardness. If social norms signify group membership and belonging, awkwardness signifies a lack of both. We admire people whose manners seem effortless because their internalization of manners shows that they truly belong. And manners performed poorly can signal pretension or inauthenticity, an attempt to claim an identity one hasn't earned. Style can be built into the requirements of etiquette itself. In the Confucian tradition, "the 'steps' etiquette prescribes incorporate expectations involving demeanor, tone . . . and most generally, aesthetic features of human comportment." Through these stylized modes of expression, we signify not only knowledge of the rule, but internalization of "the deep moral-emotional values etiquette symbolically represents" (Olberding 2016: 434–435). Awkwardness is aesthetically aversive, at least in part, because it indicates a lack of social commitment, as evidenced by a failure to fully internalize the relevant norm.

Fluency with social norms signifies a reliable potential cooperator, someone who can be counted on to know the rules and behave accordingly. By this logic, awkwardness presents the afflicted person as a social threat: not an overtly hostile one, but a flaky, unreliable one. We don't want to ally ourselves with someone who displays awkwardness, because that person has shown that they're not really "from here." Worse, they're not really from anywhere. They don't seem to know their role, or our rules—or anyone else's. This is the difference between someone who confidently behaves according to a different script and someone who awkwardly tries and fails to behave according to our scripts—the first person is rude, or deviant; the second person is awkward and hard to place. To be awkward is to be hesitant in a socially damning way. It's not that the awkward person is confidently strolling around following a different set of norms, operating with different manners—rather, they're uncertainly attempting to belong, but failing. They're not really "committed to the bit" that is etiquette. And this lack of commitment, more than a conflicting set of manners, is what damns them in our eyes.

Rudeness has long functioned as a show of power, so the claim that fluency with good manners confers social standing might sound dated or outright false. More recently, as nerdiness has become cool, being awkward has itself become a status signifier. Tech CEOs present themselves as willfully socially obtuse, and this is taken as a sign of intelligence, much as Mr. Darcy's unwillingness to attend to the social niceties of parties and dances signifies his intellectual superiority in Austen's *Pride and Prejudice*. Here, indifference to awkwardness is taken to indicate that one is so far removed from trivialities like social niceties that one couldn't possibly be bothered with them; one's mind is presumably occupied by more important matters. This is (often, though not always) an affected awkwardness—awkwardness as social flex. If that's right, it seems to undermine my claim that awkwardness is socially maladaptive since in these cases, awkwardness is a claim to status.

In fact, these are the exceptions that prove the rule. Much like a peacock's unwieldy tail, an awkward demeanor is something only an extremely "fit" individual could drag around. A willingness to appear socially awkward—or achieving success despite appearing awkward, willingly or not—telegraphs that one is extremely good at one's job. The awkward CEO isn't coasting on superficial charm; only someone whose skills speak for themselves could be so successful despite being so bad at managing social interaction.[9] The person who telegraphs awkwardness yet achieves success shows

---

[9] For example, take Elizabeth Holmes, whose startup Theranos scammed investors out of millions of dollars. Holmes aped many of the more eccentric personality traits associated with startup founders—Jobs's black turtlenecks, an affected style of speech, and an apparent social ineptitude. There's been speculation she's a sociopath; regardless, I would argue that this is an attempt at costly signaling gone awry, given her spectacular downfall. Interestingly, her demeanor and appearance at trial revealed a very different social presentation.

that they're not relying on social skills or connections: they have no need to be liked. And this is, paradoxically, a kind of confidence. Our aversion to awkwardness is mirrored by our attraction to effortlessness. True skill involves a kind of disappearing act: from the Chinese *wu-wei*, or "nonaction," to the Italian *sprezzatura*,[10] we admire the ability to conceal effort, or even escape it altogether, while executing our social performance. "No effort, no hesitation, no clumsiness of movement must intrude, in spite of the fact that table manners ... have always set out to make eating not easier but (until the techniques are mastered) more difficult" (Visser 1991: 73). Historically, this emphasis on effortless performance functioned as a form of exclusion. Visser ties it to aristocratic anxieties about encroachment by the "nouveau riche": "It was essential that those outside the pale should not be able simply to *learn* the social skills required to be 'accepted'" (1991: 71). Awkwardness is all self-conscious effort: it's clumsy and concerted, laying bare our reliance on steps and scripts. On the other hand, *wu wei* or "nonaction is action that is non-self-conscious yet perfectly responsive to the situation" (Van Norden 2011: 129). Nguyen's (2020) discussion of the aesthetics of action is also illuminating here, since effortlessness is pleasurable not only to observe but to experience: we appreciate the aesthetic qualities of our actions from inside as well as outside, taking pleasure in performing a skillful bit of knifework. If there's an aesthetic quality to smooth, uninterrupted activities, the reverse is true, too: awkwardness is aesthetically displeasing as well as socially disruptive.

That's because awkwardness signifies a lack of fluency and a lack of certainty, both of which can also signal a lack of commitment: as we noted above, the awkward person isn't sure which manners are

---

[10] For discussion of *wu wei*, see Slingerland 2015 and Van Norden 2011. For discussion of *sprezzatura*, see Visser 1991. The term is usually credited to Castaglione's sixteenth-century *Book of the Courtier*; the author describes true grace as "to practice in all things a certain nonchalance [*sprezzatura*] so as to conceal all art and make whatever is said and done appear without effort."

in play or how to execute them. And since norms depend on people's beliefs as well as their actions, the uncertainty and hesitation that awkwardness suggests is infectious and undermining: it threatens social norms and accountability by hinting at a lack of commitment. The tendency to equate social fluency with trustworthiness may have originated in response to the evolutionary challenge of identifying reliable cooperators; Dunbar (2004) suggests that dialects emerge as a way of managing worries about free-riders, with dialect functioning as a marker of in-group status. Regardless of the evolutionary explanation, it's clear that manners serve to distinguish between insiders and outsiders, and this is where the darker side of awkwardness starts to emerge: just as an emphasis on manners helped French aristocrats distinguish those "born into" a certain level of society and keep out social aspirants, our perceptions of effort or disfluency as awkwardness can, when attached to a person, function as a form of ostracism. In the second half of this chapter, I look more closely at the relationship between awkwardness, identity, and social norms.

3.3 Awkwardness and Social Norms

In the remainder of this chapter, I start to make the case for the normative significance of awkwardness. I begin by explaining how awkwardness complicates our judgments about which norms are in play, and our attempts to hold people accountable for violations of those norms, by connecting the experience of awkwardness to our beliefs about others' attitudes. I've already argued that awkwardness reflects our lack of social script, so there's a straightforward connection in that respect: awkwardness signals where our social infrastructure is inadequate or absent. But the connection goes beyond that, and awkwardness isn't always epistemically beneficial. When a topic is awkward, it's hard to get information about others' attitudes. Thus, awkwardness is an epistemic double blow: by stopping us from discussing topics, it stops us from gathering the information about others' expectations needed to determine which norms govern the issue. So even as awkwardness signifies an absence, it impedes our attempts to remedy it.

I'll say more about the way I'm thinking of social norms in a moment, but first, an example will help make the problem clearer. Many people find it awkward to talk about salary with friends or coworkers--one article compares asking someone's salary to "asking to see them naked" (Menza 2018). This is partly because we're unsure whether we are allowed to, or whether we'd be transgressing some sort of social norm were we to do so. The perception that it's awkward means that we don't know how to approach the conversation, because we've never had it, never watched someone else have it, and never been told how we should handle it. And without bringing up the topic, it is difficult to know whether others would, in fact, be offended by discussing it. But many people would benefit from greater transparency about salary: the secrecy around the issue is part of the reason that women continue to be systematically underpaid compared to men.[11]

In chapter 1, I described how scripts guide our everyday behavior by embedding norms that prescribe the sequence of events and the roles and behavior of actors. Here, I look more closely at these norms and how they are supported or undermined by awkwardness: if social scripts cue and encode norms, what happens to norms and accountability when we don't--or can't--coordinate on a script? I start by saying a bit more about what norms are and how we come to know about them.

3.3.1 Social Norms

There are various ways to taxonomize norms, but for our purposes we can think of them as occupying a spectrum from the descriptive on one end, to full-blown moral norms on the other. "Descriptive"

---

[11] See Kim 2015; Baker et al. 2023.

norms describe what people do: drive on the left, wear black to funerals, place the knife on the right. We base our beliefs about descriptive norms on information about others' behavior, rather than on beliefs about our own or others' normative attitudes. In other words, to know whether a descriptive norm is in play, all I need to do is know what others are doing. This is just one way of characterizing the distinction; in fact, taxonomies and terminologies abound, and I won't survey the various accounts here.[12]

In fact, matters are more complicated, since even if descriptive norms begin life as normatively neutral, they don't necessarily remain that way. One of the lessons we can take from our discussion of scripts in chapter 1 is that behavioral regularities tend to become normative: the fact that events usually unfold in a certain pattern leads us to form expectations that the pattern will continue, and those expectations in turn become something we feel entitled to. Moreover, we tend to conform to descriptive norms even where there's no obvious normative pressure to do so—perhaps because the regularity itself takes on the appearance of normativity, or because we take the regularity to reveal some underlying reason for the behavior and decide to imitate it (Bicchieri 2006: 64; 2008: 232). Despite these complications, we can recognize variations within the normative domain, with some norms being more or less tied to others' normative judgments versus their actions: driving on the right is something we do fairly indifferently, whereas gift-giving and the corresponding practice of writing thank-you notes is more deeply embedded in a set of social expectations and reactive attitudes.

---

[12] Bicchieri 2006, 2016; Elster 1989, 1994; Brennan et al. 2013; Kelly & Davis 2018. The terminology in these discussions varies: Lewis (1969) gives a formal analysis of conventions as the solution to coordination problems, but as Bicchieri (2006: 38–39) points out, "what is a convention to some is a social norm to others," so even if we are able to draw neat distinctions in theory, these end up complicated in practice. Bicchieri distinguishes conventions from descriptive norms; Brennan et al. eschew the label "descriptive norm" altogether, in favor of "social norm" and "convention." In writing this section, I've tried to avoid overburdening the reader with terminological distinction and explanation.

My goal here is not to defend a specific account of social norms. For the purposes of discussion, I will adopt Bicchieri's (2006, 2016) account of social norms, though I won't discuss it in detail. The important features of the account, for our purposes, are that social norms combine empirical and normative expectations. More specifically, a social norm is one that we follow because we expect others to follow it, and because we think others have the attitude that it ought to be followed. In other words, we expect that if someone doesn't follow the norm, they'll be met with disapprobation, sanctioning, or both. One implication of this is that our beliefs about which social norms are in effect are sensitive to evidence about people's behavior and to evidence about people's attitudes. Social norms play (at least) two important roles: they ground our practices of holding one another accountable, and they create and reinforce group identities. In the rest of this section, I focus on accountability; later in the chapter, I discuss identity.

3.3.2 Awkwardness, Norms, and Accountability

Awkwardness plays an epistemic role, signaling areas where social norms are unclear or absent, or where a script might be inadequate or insufficiently accessible. In doing so, it also highlights the contingency of our social scripts, drawing our attention to possibilities for revision, reconstruction, and improvement. The point about contingency will have to wait until chapter 6. For now, I'll focus on explaining the insufficiency point and its implications. For example, norms undergoing relatively rapid change can give rise to awkward situations, and awkwardness doesn't just follow from this; it makes it salient to us—it draws our attention to normative gaps and shortcomings in our scripts. For example, the awkwardness we feel when discussing salaries reveals that we don't have a clear understanding of others' attitudes about the topic. The taboo on talking about money no longer serves us, but it's yet to be replaced by scripts that would guide us through such discussions. In this sense, awkwardness functions similarly to an emotion like embarrassment, or shame: it's an alert, telling us when there's a normative disruption. But in the case of awkwardness, the disruption isn't a violation; it's something more ambiguous—and harder to repair.

Awkwardness is also an obstacle to holding people accountable for norm violations. Norms don't create accountability by ensuring that everyone calls one another out all the time. Rather, they enable an expectation of accountability such that when someone is called out, it's not strange, surprising, or awkward. Another way to put this is in terms of expectations: when we believe a norm is in play, we have corresponding beliefs about others' attitudes, and form expectations about how others will react to violations of that norm. When the response to a norm violation is hesitation or uncertainty, it signals something to others about the status of the norm, by manifesting a lack of commitment to holding others accountable.

Awkwardness thus indicates uncertainty about the existence or status of a norm. Sometimes it's the result of cases where norms are in transition or where it's genuinely underdetermined what the relevant norm is because there's no consensus among one's group (I say more about this in chapter 4). One example is the rapidly changing norms around masking when sick—or healthy. As mask mandates that were put in place during the early days of the COVID-19 pandemic were subsequently relaxed, it became unclear whether there was a norm around masking and, if so, what it demanded. For example, some people mask because they're sick; others, preventatively; for some, masking (or not masking) is a political statement. The lack of a clear norm regarding mask-wearing made it awkward to wear one, because it became unclear what the act communicated: why is the person wearing one? What judgment are they making, or intending to convey, about people who don't wear them? A headline in *The Atlantic* from summer of 2022 declared, "It's Gotten Awkward to Wear a Mask." The awkwardness signals that to the extent there ever were such norms, they are rapidly dissolving, if not dissolved.[13] The issue is further complicated by the mixed signals we get: many shops still have stickers announcing that masks are required, despite being full of unmasked employees and shoppers.[14]

Where norms are unclear, so, too, are the bases and mechanisms of accountability. If there are no norms governing seating at department meetings, it seems odd for my colleague to judge me for sitting in a certain location. If someone were to verbally chastise me for taking a certain seat, they'd look like a jerk, because I'm free to sit anywhere. But now suppose that while there are no explicit rules about seating, the department chair always sits at the head of the table as a matter of habit. Being new, I don't know this; I enter before her and sit in "her" seat. Now things may get awkward, because it's unclear (a) whether there is in fact a norm that this is "the chair's seat" and (b) whose job it is to enforce it. Indeed, in this case, the ambiguity of the norm and my relation to it marks me out as not-quite-a-member-of-the-department; it also forces my colleagues to consider whether the department is in fact committed to such a norm.

This relatively benign (and purely fictional) example shows two things: first, it illustrates how stealthily descriptive regularities can become normative. Second, it illustrates that this normativity can go undetected until it's breached, at which point the question of accountability forces us to make a decision about our commitment or lack thereof. However, if we haven't considered our normative expectations (or others'), then not only might we lack a belief

---

[13] Of course, by the time this is published, the norms may have shifted yet again, making the example here outdated. But this only shows how quickly our norms can shift, giving rise to (and resolving) awkwardness around an issue.

[14] One way to put it is that in this case, we're getting mixed descriptive and "injunctive" cues. Cialdini et al. (1990) use the term "injunctive" to describe norms or norm-relevant information that invokes normative attitudes or judgments, rather than information about what people are actually doing. So, a sign that says "no littering" is injunctive; watching a person drop a flyer on the floor is descriptive. I've tried not to overburden the reader with terminology, so I've stuck with Bicchieri's categories of normative and empirical expectations instead.

about them, but they may be genuinely underdetermined. It's unlikely anyone involved in this hypothetical scenario would explicitly avow a norm about seating, but the practice comes to function like one, whether we realize it or not. Once this fact becomes salient, we're forced to decide whether we endorse the norm or not, via the choice to enforce it, to criticize someone else for enforcing it, and so on. And this is where things can become awkward, as we have to choose whether to commit to the norm without explicitly negotiating or deliberating—because social interactions move fast.

Of course, the choice not to enforce a norm isn't always so benign: interviewed in an article about why men don't intervene in cases of workplace harassment, one man admitted that though he knew his coworkers sometimes looked at pornography while at work, and held meetings at strip clubs, "I was friendly with the guys and I knew it would be really awkward if I confronted them" (Tsoulis-Reay 2017). The problem here isn't this man's uncertainty about the norms in play at his workplace. He knows that what his coworkers are doing is wrong. But the silence caused by his desire to avoid an awkward interaction with coworkers effectively undermines the norm against such behaviors, by undermining the perception of accountability.

Uncertainty about others' normative expectations is one source of ambiguity about which norms are in play. Another source comes from scripts themselves, because while we typically aren't aware of "choosing" a script to apply to a situation—part of what makes scripts so useful is the effortlessness with which they're typically activated—we sometimes have options about how to classify actors and events. And the choices we make affect the norms to which others are held accountable—or not.

3.4 Norms, Scripts, and Roles

The classifications provided by scripts scaffold our normative expectations. Being able to bring the appropriate normative expectations to a situation requires first classifying the situation as belonging to one type or another. For example, activating the "lecture" script cues an associated set of norms; this gives us hints both about how we're expected to behave, and about which behaviors we're entitled to expect from others. If others' behavior is discordant enough, we might shift our belief about what kind of event is unfolding. This means there's an interplay between our descriptive classification and the normative expectations associated with the script—an event that departs significantly from a number of elements of the lecture script might be a really bad lecture, or a really good cocktail party. In other words, we have the option of shifting our normative assessment, or shifting our classification of the event, person, or role (he's not a jerk, he's an awkward genius!).

This link between the empirical and normative components means that we can shift our normative assessment of a situation or action by shifting our descriptive classification, and the ambiguity of awkwardness lends itself to such shifts. Confronted with an awkward situation, we can dissolve the awkwardness by altering our expectations about which norm is at play in a given situation ("in this industry, it's normal to go out drinking with your colleagues"), or by altering our classification of a behavior ("he was probably joking"). Witness the frequency with which problematic or rude behavior is written off as "merely" socially awkward, and even a sign of intelligence: "Silicon Valley fetishizes a particular type of engineer—young, male, awkward, unattached . . . any callousness on his part towards women can be excused by the catchall term 'awkwardness.'" But this trope, which we encountered earlier in section 3.2, is not equally available to everyone: "women, by the same token, are expected to fill in for men's awkwardness with exceptional social skills . . . he is 'too focused on work' and his 'awkwardness' is a sign of genius" (Losse 2014).

Shifting someone's role shifts the normative expectations to which they're held; intentionally or not, this can be a way of letting them off the hook for their behavior. (I'll come back to the intersection of awkwardness and gender in chapter 5.) The troubled, moody artist; the socially awkward tech worker (or philosopher); the temperamental power broker: these roles, and the scripts we associate with them, are ripe for exploitation. Activating a particular script might seem like a descriptive exercise, as if the script is "triggered" by the environment and we're along for the ride. But we can exercise control here: as we saw in chapter 1, scripts are "consensual" insofar as my ability to enact one depends on others' willingness to play along; which script gets triggered depends in part on how we agree to classify aspects of our environment. And our choices have consequences, because the way we classify people or events—afternoon meeting or happy hour? artist or professor?—determines the norms to which we hold each other accountable.

3.4.1 Awkwardness and Pluralistic Ignorance

While even descriptive regularities can become normative by virtue of giving rise to expectations, we can distinguish different kinds of information relevant to a norm's existence, maintenance, and revision. Some norms rely on information about what others are doing. Others rely on information about what others are thinking—their normative attitudes and expectations—where this might differ from what we observe them doing. This type of norm can be harder to dislodge; awkwardness is one reason why.

Before I explain, note that awkwardness is an obstacle to accessing even empirical information about others' behavior. If my empirical belief about which side of the road people drive on is false, I'll find out pretty quickly (and dramatically). But it's harder for me to access information about other people's sex lives and bodily functions. At the risk of stating the obvious, when we anticipate that talking about something will be awkward, we're less likely to discuss it. And this creates ambiguity about both what the actual norm is, as we saw above, and what people would prefer it to be, as we'll see below.

In practice, it can be difficult to distinguish cases where we lack a script and therefore anticipate that a subject will be awkward (maybe because we've had awkward experiences trying to raise the issue in the past) from cases where there's a norm against speaking about the issue. That's one lesson of the salary example above. This is significant, because false beliefs about others' normative expectations enable social norms to remain in effect even when we'd rather they didn't (Bicchieri 2006; Brennan et al. 2013).

Our reluctance to discuss both normative and empirical expectations hinders norm change. It's possible that everyone prefers to have a different norm, and that in fact people are already conforming to a different norm empirically, but because of a lack of discussion we don't realize it. We lack scripts for talking about certain issues—bodily functions, money, sex—in part because we don't discuss them, so we can't gather evidence about other people's attitudes. As a result, we may falsely conclude that people endorse the silence we observe around the issue. I say more about why this is problematic in section 4.5, but the important point for our purposes here is that silence is ambiguous, and can lead to false perceptions of consensus.

These failures to discuss our attitudes put us on shaky epistemic ground, for two reasons. First, we're in a poor epistemic position with respect to the issue in general: when it's awkward to broach a topic, we lack the epistemic resources provided by others' experiences and attitudes. Examples range from people's lived experiences of race and racism, to physical experiences of postpartum recovery and menopause. I say more about this problem in chapter 5. The second reason is more specific to norms themselves: when we don't talk about our attitudes, we risk making mistaken inferences about what others think and prefer. We might think that others disapprove of the behavior in question, or of discussing it, when they don't; our own silence might lead them to make the same mistaken inference about us. Here the problem isn't how to change people's normative attitudes, but how to get more accurate information about them. This is the problem of pluralistic ignorance, and it is one reason why norms persist even when everyone would prefer a different norm—the belief that people are content with the current arrangement prevents any shift from taking place. We can already see where awkwardness is going to enter the picture: by making it hard to discuss certain issues, awkwardness blocks us from sharing information about others' expectations, thus contributing to pluralistic ignorance.

A familiar example of pluralistic ignorance involves class participation: students notice that no one is asking questions in class, so they assume everyone understands the material except them, and they're too embarrassed to ask a question. Meanwhile, everyone else is thinking the same thing and feeling the same way (Prentice & Miller 1996: 162). But in this case, information about others' normative attitudes won't suffice to shift things—it's not enough for the professor to give students normative permission to ask questions, or even for students to believe that other students endorse asking questions. What students need is the empirical information that their peers are just as confused as they are.

Another example involves attitudes toward drinking: studies suggest that college students often overestimate other students' alcohol use while misjudging their attitudes toward alcohol. So, many colleges discourage binge drinking via campaigns aimed at counteracting this misconception, for example, with posters informing students that binge drinking is actually infrequent and that most students consume little if any alcohol. These campaigns directly target pluralistic ignorance, taking advantage of the fact that students want to conform with their peers (Sanderson 2020; see also Prentice & Miller 1993). Their messaging is aimed both at changing beliefs about what others are doing, and reinforcing the targets' identities as members of a particular group: Hamilton College students, "Boston Strong," and so on. In the next section, I look more closely at the relationship between awkwardness and identity: how does our access to social scripts affect our ability to hold others accountable? How does being vulnerable to awkwardness mark one as an outsider, and how do the scripts available to us determine the roles we're able to occupy?

3.5 Awkwardness, Identity, and Exclusion

Anderson (2000: 191) suggests, "The great puzzle of social norms is not why people obey them.... It is, how do shared standards of conduct acquire their normativity to begin with?" Her answer: the normativity of social norms arises out of our membership in a group whose identity is constituted in part by those norms. To understand the norm as normative is part of what it *is* to be a member of the group; the collective is constituted, in part, by an agreement to regard one another as accountable, and to hold one another accountable, to (among other things) obeying those same norms (Brennan et al. 2013).

The link between norms, roles, and group membership reveals another reason for our aversion to awkwardness: it threatens our claims to belonging. When situations get awkward, it's because someone doesn't know how things are done. And if accountability to certain norms is part of what underwrites the group's existence, then ambiguity about those norms, or about who's accountable to them (and who's entitled to hold them accountable) poses an existential threat. Group membership, identity, and the need to belong provide additional motivations to comply with norms and perform the roles offered to us.

Nor is the motivation to perform always external. Enacting a script is a performance, and like most performances, we may take pleasure in pulling it off successfully, even if we're not particularly invested in the script itself. For example, when my husband and I go to the local hardware store, we find ourselves enacting a script I deplore: the beleaguered husband and nagging wife. Each time, I tell myself I will not play this role; each time, the owner of the shop somehow corrals us into a repeat performance. What strikes me about it is that even as I deplore the script itself, I recognize the fact that it's allowing me to become someone the other person recognizes—I take on the role that's offered to me rather than risk being marked out as an anomaly. We don't have to endorse scripts in order to feel bound to them. As the example here shows, we sometimes prefer to adhere to a script we don't endorse than be left with no script at all. Displaying knowledge of the group's norms, and competence with them, is a way of showing that one belongs. So is having a role to play in the scripts: it lets us demonstrate that we belong and it helps others "locate" the relevant norms that apply to us. To put it another way, if others don't know what role we're playing, they don't know how to treat us—or what to expect from us. As Manne (2018: 169) notes, "part of being recognized as human involves the potential to be cast in social scripts in specific roles and relations," such that the failure to cooperate or fit with a script—or perhaps worse, the failure to be "castable," in a recognizable role—makes one vulnerable to ostracism, rejection, and reprisal.

Notice how quickly we moved from a relatively trivial example (going to a hardware store) to a drastic conclusion (social ostracism). That's the point: apparently trivial choices, practices, and encounters can lead to moments of discomfort, ostracism, and awkwardness that are anything but. This shows that having access to social scripts confers a significant social benefit; lacking them, or failing to be cast in a role, incurs a significant social cost.

3.5.1 Awkwardness and Identity

Awkwardness is closely linked to identity: what "makes someone awkward,"[15] and what makes that awkwardness aversive or objectionable, depends on who we take that person to be and how they

---

[15] The quotes here should be read as indicating that I don't endorse this phrase, for reasons laid out in chapter 1. I use it to describe a kind of judgment we sometimes make about people, not to claim that the judgment is accurate or warranted.

identify themselves. Some identities—toddler, tech CEO—are more insulated from awkwardness than others. What makes a situation awkward is not the individuals involved, but the interaction between individuals and scripts, an interaction which is mediated by the various identities we inhabit. Bringing the wrong self to a performance, needing to perform two selves at once, or encountering a clash between one's identities and one's scripted role(s) can all make it difficult or impossible for someone to "perform" correctly, forcing them into awkward situations. How we interpret the self someone brings to an interaction affects which scripts we see them as fitting into; this in turn affects whether their actions are interpreted as awkward or uncooperative, depending on the expectations cued by our script.

If social norms maintain groups and identities, then failing to make these norms clear to others has the effect of denying them full group membership. Our identities are formed in part by our membership in various groups—our families, workplaces, social and religious associations, and so on. And these groups are delimited, in part, by norms. To be a full-fledged group member is to know what those norms are: what others expect from us, and what we're entitled to expect from others. Denying someone this information also excludes them from decisions about accountability: because the norm is ambiguous or unknown, they don't know who if anyone is accountable to it, or who is entitled to hold others accountable. A philosophy student describes the disorientation he felt when trying to report a famous faculty member for sexual harassment:

> I was made to feel like some kind of weirdo, for thinking we needed to talk about what had happened and have more transparency. . . . This was disorienting. I had to update my understanding of "how the world works." I started to find it difficult to develop and sustain trusting professional relationships.[16]

---

[16] https://dailynous.com/2021/07/19/blowing-the-whistle-on-john-searle/

I've focused on how our ignorance of scripts and norms affects how others appraise us and our belonging, but it has first-person effects, too. The feeling that one doesn't belong or know how things are done "around here" doesn't confine itself to seating choices; it may recur as worries about whether one's teaching evaluations are subject to gender bias, whether one is misunderstanding someone's jokes, or whether what one is witnessing counts as harassment.

Withholding scripts from others is a form of social exclusion. This exclusion can be the result of bias, whether explicit or implicit; it can be intentional or accidental. For example, first-generation college students often lack the "hidden curriculum" that contains scripts about office hours, how to study, extracurricular opportunities and expectations, forms of communication with faculty and other students, and so on.[17] In this case, we recognize exclusionary scripts as a problem that can and should be remedied; institutions and educators work to make its norms and scripts more explicit and available. Informational campaigns also highlight the identity of "first-generation" students and faculty (in other words, the first generation in one's family to attend college), thereby offering students membership in a group that doesn't assume knowledge of those scripts. This in turn highlights the contingency of norms and scripts such as the ones governing office hours, or composing an email to faculty: lack of facility with these doesn't make a person awkward (or a bad student); it means they haven't acquired the script yet.

But while making scripts explicit means that more people have access to them, it doesn't mean we get to choose which one we perform on any given occasion. The roles available to us depend not only on the scripts we hold, but on the overlap between these and the scripts held by others. I would prefer not to play the role of the nagging wife, and my husband would prefer not to play the role of

---

[17] Semper & Blasco 2018; see also the essays collected in Margolis 2001.

the beleaguered husband. But we would both prefer to play those roles for a few minutes to enduring a few minutes of awkwardness. That's a trade-off we often make—opting to "play along" rather than make things awkward.

In other cases, the choice isn't up to us. For example, philosophical argumentation has historically rewarded a certain type of assertiveness—aggressiveness, even—that's at odds with the deferential, friendly, and warm behavior often expected of women in the workplace.[18] Conflicting expectations like these can make it difficult if not impossible for a woman to successfully perform her role—especially because these sorts of expectations can lead to increased self-monitoring, which in turn produces the self-consciousness and hesitance we associate with awkwardness and precludes the effortlessness we associate with confidence and status, as we saw in our discussion of manners in section 3.2.2 (Pontari & Schlenker, 2000).

Goffman describes an encounter between two "differently placed" members of a workplace in the elevator (which he identifies as a prime locus of embarrassment). The men in Goffman's scenario are not on chatting terms, but they are placed in a context which demands small talk. Goffman describes the ensuing embarrassment[19] as a sacrifice made by the individual on behalf of social order: "Social structure gains elasticity; the individual merely loses composure" (1956: 271). A similar point might be made about awkwardness, but often, there's nothing "mere" about it; the loss of composure can be felt quite keenly, and how others respond to our presence in an elevator depends not only on our social role, but on our identity, our race and gender—a point illustrated in a very different passage about elevators, Yancy's description of the "elevator effect"—what it's like to be a Black man in an elevator with a white woman. In the elevator, Yancy is no longer a professor in a

[18] Moulton 1983; Beebee 2013; Saul 2013; Kidd 2016.
[19] I'm following Goffman in using "embarrassment" here, though for the reasons outlined in chapter 2, I think the case is better described in terms of awkwardness.

suit: "Over and above how my body is clothed, she 'sees' a criminal, she sees me as a threat. Independently of any threatening action on my part, my Black body, my existence in Black, poses a threat" (2008: 846). Yancy's example reminds us that the ability to occupy different selves in different situations, and to decide which self we bring to which occasion, is not limitless; nor is it equally limited for everyone. And the costs imposed by the trade-off Goffman describes—in which the individual sacrifices their own composure and face on behalf of "social structure"—are not equally borne.[20]

Goffman's suggestion that we perform different selves for different occasions offers a way of thinking about our everyday interactions that's both helpful and potentially misleading. It helps illuminate the awkwardness that ensues when we're not sure which self to bring to an interaction, or when we bring the wrong one. But it's misleading insofar as it tempts us to think of awkwardness as the result of failed or inept individual performances. This is true of the script metaphor more generally: by explaining awkwardness as emerging out of the absence or failure of a script, we risk seeing it as a function of an individual's possession of, or competence with, a social script.

But our performances and even identities are determined in part by the scripts available to us. One reason we find ourselves without a script is that we want to convey one meaning without another, but we can't find a way of doing so. For example, we want to be supportive but critical; we want to be perceived as authoritative but also caring; we want to stick to our food ethics while being good guests. I'll say more about these issues and how we navigate them in chapter 4. But notice that in these cases, awkwardness arises not because of conflicting norms, but because of conflicts within

---

[20] Notably, Goffman suggests that cafeterias and elevators segregated by status are a way to avoid such "embarrassing" encounters; the "democratic orientation" of "newer establishments" exacerbates it. We may see echoes of this desire to avoid reminders of class difference in the controversial practice, adopted by some New York City mixed-income housing developments, of having separate entrances for low-income residents.

or between scripts: it feels impossible to perform one role without excluding the other. Because the social significance of our actions isn't up to us, we can have trouble disentangling their normative implications. This isn't always a bad thing—an older male boss might be unable to comment on his female subordinate's vacation pictures without coming across as creepy.[21] That's fine. Other cases are more problematic: a female graduate student wants to prove her argumentative skills in a highly combative department without coming across as a "bitch," but because our assessments of argumentative performance are gender-biased, she's unable to do so.

The problem here isn't just that we dislike the existing scripts—though that is a problem, and it requires us to think in terms of conceptual engineering, a point I discuss in chapter 6. It's that it feels difficult to do one thing without also doing the other, and we sometimes lack the resources to communicate this difficulty; what we communicate isn't entirely up to us. Perversely, sometimes insisting that we don't intend some meaning only seems to reinforce the idea that we do (a prime example is our tendency to preface statements with "no offense"). I'll say more about speech in chapter 5. Here, the point is more general: scripts constrain the roles available to us and the performances we're able to carry out. By imbuing certain actions, emotional expressions, and utterances with additional meanings, our scripts prevent us from communicating certain things, or leave our meaning ambiguous.

3.6 Conclusion

In the last chapter, I looked at how awkwardness felt from the inside. Here, I've described what it looks like from outside, and what it tells others about us. We've seen how awkwardness undermines individual identities, group norms, and accountability.

---

[21] For discussion of a related example, see Kukla 2014.

Awkwardness can undermine social norms; it can also call our attention to areas where they're lacking, offering opportunities for improvement. It can deter us from holding others accountable, and offer some people an excuse for bad behavior even as it places additional demands on others. I'll come back to the ways awkwardness reinforces inequalities in chapter 5. In the next chapter, I explore awkwardness's inhibitory role in more detail.

4
Morally Awkward Problems

4.1 Introduction: The Other Milgram Experiment

In 1974, Stanley Milgram sent his graduate students into the New York City subways to "violate a residual rule and observe the consequences." Specifically, they were instructed to approach sitting passengers and ask for their seat. This turned out to be more difficult than expected: anticipating the consequences was so unpleasant that many students couldn't bring themselves to follow instructions. Milgram and Sabini report:

> Most students reported extreme difficulty in carrying out the assignment. Students reported that when standing in front of a subject they felt anxious, tense, and embarrassed. Frequently, they were unable to vocalize the request for a seat and had to withdraw. They sometimes feared that they were at the center of attention of the car and were often unable to look directly at the subject. (1978: 37)

The first graduate student sent out managed to complete 14 of the 20 assigned trials. Milgram later recalled that confronted with the discrepancy, his student confessed, "I just couldn't go on. It was one of the most difficult things I ever did in my life." Determined to carry out the task himself, Milgram "assumed it would be easy," but on approaching the seated passenger, he reported, "the words seemed lodged in my trachea and simply would not emerge . . .

I was overwhelmed by paralyzing inhibition ... stark anomic panic overcame me" (Tavris 1974: 72).

Given that Milgram is best known for documenting obedience, there's a certain irony here. And in this case, no one was required to deliver painful electric shocks—just make a straightforward request which subjects were free to refuse. The moral of the story: social norms create powerful inhibitions. They can prevent us from doing what we think we should, and what have good reason to do, even when we don't consciously endorse the inhibiting norm or expect it to influence us.

I'll come back to the relative priority of social and moral norms later in this chapter. But first, I'll take up a different issue involving the inhibitory power of awkwardness. So far, I've focused on awkwardness as a social phenomenon, an instrument of social influence or ostracism. In the next chapter, I'll argue that it plays a significant role in producing and maintaining social and epistemic injustice. Here, I argue for a more direct relationship between awkwardness and morality: awkwardness inhibits us from moral criticism and moral action.

I identify what I call "morally awkward problems": issues that cross-cut categories, leaving it unclear which script is appropriate for dealing with them. This category includes issues that lack a clear status as either moral or personal; it also includes issues where the norms for criticism or intervention are unclear, because the issue is unsettled, we don't know what others' expectations are, or we're unsure how to convey the meaning we want. Morally awkward problems provide insight into the sources of uncertainty and ambiguity in our everyday moral lives. These uncertainties create opportunities for awkwardness, as we seek (unsuccessfully) to classify issues and situations as moral or social. I'll focus on two types of cases: bystander cases, which are a familiar staple of the literature on situationism and moral psychology, and (failures of) moral criticism, which are less familiar, but nonetheless an important feature of our everyday moral lives.

I start by asking why we don't engage in moral critique more often. This might seem like a non-issue, either because there's no reason to think we should engage in it to begin with, or because awkwardness is the wrong place to look for an explanation of why we don't. After addressing the first set of worries, I show why I think awkwardness offers an explanation by pointing to another, related phenomenon: the bystander effect. While some researchers have argued that the bystander effect can be explained by embarrassment, I'll argue that both the bystander effect and the self-silencing of moral critique are the result of moral ambiguity—in other words, these are morally awkward problems.

4.2 The Problem of Moral Critique

A woman worries about her coworker's racist comments: she should say something to correct them, but she doesn't want to make things awkward around the office. At the height of the COVID-19 pandemic, a doctor attends a gathering where few guests are wearing masks; not only does he not comment on others' lack of masks, he contemplates taking off his own—that's how awkward he feels wearing it (Klitzman 2020). A tenured professor of psychology describes her interactions with a male colleague:

> I enjoyed his company. But on a few occasions he made comments that felt somewhat inappropriate. Once he noted that I'd lost weight and said I "looked really good." On another occasion he suggested that if I was ever lonely on a business trip, I should let him know and he'd come with me. These comments consistently made me uncomfortable, but I never mustered the courage to tell him to cut it out. . . . I was a tenured professor, and he had no power over my career . . . yet I said nothing. . . . I didn't want to make things awkward between us. (Sanderson 2020: 65–66)

Seen one way, this is puzzling: we know that racism, pandemics and disease, and sexual harassment are significant moral problems. How does our desire to avoid transient social awkwardness override the opportunity to act on some of our deepest moral concerns? That's the question that motivates this chapter. I begin by addressing some alternative explanations that don't rely on awkwardness: maybe there is no reason we should critique one another; maybe we already critique a lot. I offer some reasons why engaging in moral critique is important, and differs from preventing wrongdoing. Part of the explanation involves distinguishing ways of engaging in moral critique, and understanding the different meanings that criticism can carry. I'll argue that we lack the social scripts we need to engage in interpersonal moral criticism, and as a result, we engage in a kind of self-silencing. I then show how altering the meaning we associate with criticism could make it less awkward to engage in within friendships and personal relationships.

A couple of caveats: first, as will become clear in the discussion below, my target here is not the question of whether we should *blame* people for certain moral choices or behaviors. The kind of criticism I'm interested in is compatible with a variety of views about their blameworthiness and our entitlement to blame. In practice, criticism and blame may be hard to disentangle: one may feel a lot like the other. That's part of my point here, and part of what I think makes the issue so difficult. Second, I'm framing the issue here in terms of speech. But there's a broader "puzzle of accommodation," which involves questions about why we do things like split the dinner check with meat-eating friends if we believe meat-eating is wrong (Harman 2016). Insofar as actions that amount to refusals to accommodate also express disapproval, and would presumably be read as criticism (and require some kind of explanation), the considerations discussed below apply to them as well. I start by anticipating some objections to how I've framed the problem of criticism. While the discussion and examples that follow assume certain normative views and commitments, readers who reject the issues I've chosen as examples should feel free to substitute their own.

4.2.1 Objection 1: Reasons for Withholding Criticism

One might question whether there is a problem here at all: perhaps we actually *do* have good reasons for not criticizing in cases like the above. Some philosophers have invoked the value of autonomy in defense of the view that we should allow others to make moral mistakes or engage in moral wrongs (e.g., Waldron 1981; Doggett 2022). The thought could be that intervening curtails people's autonomy in undesirable ways—that it infringes on their rights or self-determination. Alternatively, it might be that criticism should be avoided because any real change in moral attitude or behavior should come not from external social pressure, but from the agent herself.

While autonomy and moral intervention may sometimes conflict, this is more of a concern in cases where we're considering intervening to prevent an action. Autonomy doesn't require immunity from criticism. Respecting someone's autonomy might require not preventing them from buying meat, or not demanding that they refrain from eating meat in your presence. But it doesn't require refraining from criticizing them. Indeed, it might even require criticism: if my criticism involves pointing out moral considerations they're overlooking, I may be enhancing their autonomy by ensuring that they make a fully informed decision. Criticism can be a way of showing respect for someone's moral autonomy, by treating them as responsive to reasons.

Another concern is that criticizing others' choices intrudes on their privacy by demanding reasons for their choices. Given that most people know about the environmental impacts of choices like single-use plastic or factory-farmed meat, one might argue that it's intrusive to demand they justify those choices to us. Instead, we respect people by assuming they have reasons, and allowing those reasons to remain private. This line of thought seems particularly apt with respect to food, since our food choices often involve cultural, health, and economic considerations. We might also think that friendship imposes a special obligation here: part of what it is to be a friend is to respect someone's decision-making, and to grant them a presumption of rationality, which we demonstrate by not demanding justification for their choices. Friendship involves trust and perhaps a kind of epistemic reliance:

> When we depend on a friend to bear authentic and reliable witness to her moral experience, we are trusting . . . the quality of her sensitivity and insightfulness into her own life. We rely on the friend to have noticed what is significant about the circumstances which she faced, and we rely on her to have conceptualized that significance in appropriate terms. (Friedman 1989: 10)

Being friends doesn't mean never having to say you're sorry, but it might mean minimizing your requests for reasons.

Suppose none of the above considerations applies: it's not disrespectful, autonomy-reducing, or friendship-damaging to criticize others. This shows only that we're permitted to do so. But should we? Do we have any obligation to speak up when we think others are doing wrong? It might seem obvious that the answer is yes, but Doggett (2022) argues that except in cases in where the wrongdoing has a specific victim to whom we owe protection, we have no obligation to speak up or intervene. In other words, we have an obligation to stop someone from hurting a specific innocent victim; we have no obligation to step in and stop someone from not recycling, or eating factory-farmed meat. If this is right, the objections discussed above are unnecessary, because there is no obligation to begin with.

4.2.2 Objection 2: No Reason to Speak

However, my concern here is not with whether we are *obligated* to speak up to prevent wrongdoing—it's whether it *would be better* to speak up when witnessing suberogatory behavior. It's consistent with views like Doggett's that while failing to criticize doesn't violate an obligation, it would nonetheless be better if we were to engage in it.[1] It's also consistent with this view that we have an obligation to comment when we see others doing wrong, even if doing so doesn't prevent their wrongdoing: politely refraining from criticism seems to undermine a transparency or honesty on which intimate relationships depend. Alternatively, failing to speak up might make us guilty of what Driver (2015) calls "tolerance complicity" with the behavior in question: we're not participating in it, but we're not doing anything to change it, either.

Even if it's not wrong to critique others, we can justifiably worry about our qualification to do so: perhaps we're ignorant of someone's circumstances or limitations, where this knowledge would change our moral appraisal of their actions. For example, when some US grocery chains started selling pre-peeled oranges in plastic containers, the Internet was quick to respond with condemnation (and mockery). The idea seemed obviously wasteful, like it was designed to pander to consumer laziness. But others pointed out that packaging like this makes fresh fruits and vegetables accessible to those who would otherwise have trouble peeling a piece of fruit: for example, people with arthritis, chronic pain, or physical disabilities (Danovich 2016). This doesn't change the environmental cost of plastic packaging, but it does point to the potential limitations of our moral viewpoint and calculations: those who have never struggled to peel an orange might not appreciate

---

[1] From a consequentialist perspective, these may be indistinguishable: if it would be better (lead to better consequences) for me to speak up, and I don't, I've done something wrong. I'm neutral between first-order moral views here.

the considerations at work here. Likewise, we may hesitate to critique someone's food choices because we don't know the reasons for them, and we don't want to force someone into an uncomfortable disclosure: what if they're operating under financial constraints they'd rather not discuss? In fact, I'll argue that discomfort is part of the explanation here, but discomfort related to criticism and disagreement, rather than epistemic humility per se.

If epistemic limitations give us reason to hesitate before critiquing, they also provide an argument in favor of it. Being a virtuous consumer is epistemically demanding:

> [T]o demand a high level of investigation with respect to every decision we make would seem infeasible. It is not viable for us to read every report released by every environmental organization, even if each could provide us with valuable, relevant information about a host of important issues. Similarly, investigating thoroughly the origins and impacts of every individual food item we purchase, or every alternative action we could perform, while in some ways desirable, is not a plausible option for us. If such standards of information-gathering were treated as necessary for agents to be minimally virtuous, we would likely never act as we continually attempt to become better-informed, thoroughly assessing various goods, options, etc. (Kawall 2010: 110)

Engaging in moral critique offloads some of this epistemic burden onto others. If I know that my friends will step in and redirect me if I make a poor choice, or an ill-informed one, I can be more selective about where I direct my own epistemic and personal resources, investigating some goods but not others, and focusing my energy on particular projects or issues. I can develop my own areas of moral expertise and become an epistemic resource for others. Criticism can be a way to pool our epistemic resources, and an avenue through which to share them.

4.2.3 Objection 3: No Shortage of Criticism

At this point one might object that my discussion so far rests on a false presupposition: I'm claiming that we don't engage in moral critique when, in fact, we criticize people all the time. There are entire segments of the Internet devoted to picking apart people's food habits, consumer choices, and Tinder profiles. Reality television shows are scrutinized for their treatment of moral and social issues. In light of the voracity with which we engage in moral debates about everything from so-called real housewives to fake news, the premise of this chapter might seem obviously false.

The point, though, is not whether we critique others, but where and how we do so: online and impersonally, not face-to-face and friend-to-friend. So-called call-out or cancel culture typically plays out online or in more traditional forms of media (like print), and it involves ostracism rather than engagement. These kinds of criticism are often described as "shaming."[2] When we collectively and publicly judge someone, the overall effect tends to be punitive, rather than instructive (a difference we'll examine in more detail below). The whole thing plays out publicly, at the scale of the collective rather than individual relationships. And the consequences are different: while I can end a friendship over someone's racist jokes, or a misogynistic tweet of theirs, I can't "cancel" them—that requires a more collective judgment.

Public moral criticism can be harsh and destructive, and it's often derided as "virtue signaling."[3] But it's not without its uses: in chapter 3, I argued that uncertainty about others' attitudes can undermine social norms and accountability. This shows that we have reasons for engaging in moral criticism that stem from a general need to maintain norms, rather than our relationship to or

---

[2] See Ronson 2015 for a discussion of public shaming; Rini 2021, chapter 8, has a discussion of blaming and shaming on social media.
[3] For example, Tosi and Warmke 2020 refer to it as "moral grandstanding."

concern for a particular agent or agents. What about within personal relationships? Here it's useful to distinguish the kind of criticism we engage with online, or in moral debates involving hypothetical cases, from that which we give in our personal relationships. One difference is that the criticism we give friends doesn't presuppose the existence of a disagreement, and doesn't proceed like a disagreement or argument. Often, it's the opposite: I critique someone because I observe behavior out of line what I know to be shared values, as (for example) when I point out that someone's behavior is inconsistent with their commitment to sustainability.[4]

Criticism can be a way of redirecting our attention to issues that we care about, but might neglect through inattention or ignorance. Distracted by my surroundings, I fail to notice I'm ordering a dish containing dairy; in my rush to get out of the grocery store, I grab a product and throw it in my cart. Or, I don't know that organic food can still use pesticides; I don't realize that not every vendor at the farmer's market is selling locally grown food.

All of these lapses are excusable, and one might wonder whether criticism really is the best description of what we're engaged in here—perhaps it's better to characterize it as something more like "informing," or "suggesting." I don't disagree, and part of what I'm arguing for is reframing how we think about the practice of moral criticism, both as givers and recipients. However, I think "critique" is still a useful way of describing the practice, mainly because that's how we tend to experience it. If someone points out that I'm doing something wrong, or I should be doing it differently, it's often interpreted as criticizing what I'm currently doing, rather than as praise with a suggestion of how to do even better. This is especially true in cases where the behavior concerns something I care

---

[4] One might view this as a type of moral argument, or at least, moral persuasion. A certain kind of emotivist might even think this is the most we can really do in cases of moral arguments—appeal to consistency and shared values (Ayer makes comments to this effect in *Language, Truth and Logic*). But while this is consistent with disagreement, it doesn't presuppose it; it's not argument in the sense of conflict, but argument in the sense of persuasion.

about, as is the case here—if I'm borrowing a pen from your desk to sign a form, I don't have much invested in the choice. But someone buying food at the farmer's market might care a lot about making sustainable choices, and being told they're missing the mark hits differently.

4.2.4 What's Wrong with Moral Critique?

Part of what makes criticism hard to hear is that it can feel a lot like blame. But this is another mistake, which points to another way we might rewrite our scripts: not only by reframing criticism as suggestion, but by decoupling the association between criticism and responsibility. Calhoun (2016: 201) points out that we're entitled to reproach others even in contexts where we may not hold them responsible for their actions; failure to do so can be seen as sanctioning the behavior. Calhoun is particularly interested in what she calls "abnormal moral contexts": situations in which "moral ignorance is the norm" (2016: 200). She gives the example of feminist critiques of routine social practices. At first, these critiques were accessible only to a relatively confined intellectual sphere, before slowly filtering into public consciousness. In cases like these, we critique discrimination and bias even while we may not hold perpetrators accountable; we take their ignorance as excusing them from responsibility, but not as letting them off the hook from criticism. This is a particularly interesting approach in the context of food ethics and choice, since the sheer complexity of the food system renders many of its costs and effects opaque to consumers, and that's without taking into account the additional difficulty of figuring out what, exactly, one is buying or consuming.[5] If criticism

---

[5] I should clarify that this is not the kind of ignorance that Calhoun is talking about; what makes a moral context "abnormal," on her account, is specifically *moral* ignorance, where someone fails to possess the relevant moral knowledge. The kind of ignorance

and blame come apart, it opens up space for rethinking the aims of moral criticism. In other words, if we don't engage in it to assign or communicate blame, what is it for?

4.2.5 Summative versus Formative Criticism

Much of our moral evaluation is what Zheng (2021) calls *summative moral criticism*: it evaluates us by looking at whether or how well we've met some moral standard. Zheng argues for an alternative, which she calls *formative moral criticism*: it aims not at giving an evaluation of past performance, but at giving feedback that will inform and improve future performance. The moral conversations I'm interested in here involve this kind of formative criticism: critique aimed at helping "motivate, inform, and reinforce our efforts to improve" ourselves and our behavior (Zheng 2021: 513–514).[6] Whereas summative moral criticism is available to us in our capacity as moral agents, formative moral criticism is more commonly and appropriately leveraged in interpersonal contexts. I can give summative criticism of historical figures, politicians, and strangers; we deploy it in philosophical debates and in our teaching, when we evaluate hypothetical moral dilemmas and ask students to assign blame to hypothetical actors. We engage in it when we comment on forums, like Reddit's "Am I the Asshole," or while arguing in the comment threads of reality TV recaps. In short, we have a lot of experience with summative criticism. Not only is it familiar, but because it's done from a distance, there's something safe about it.

I'm describing in the food case is factual, though it's necessary for making an informed moral judgment; one might argue that ignorance of the practices involved in food production is so integral to moral judgment as to be a kind of moral ignorance, so I think the comparison is warranted.

[6] I should clarify that while I borrow the distinction from Zheng, I'm adapting it for the purposes of my argument; I don't mean to suggest she'd endorse all the claims made here or the use to which I put the distinction.

Formative criticism is different. Because it aims at helping us improve our behavior and develop better moral practices, it's likely to come from those who have an interest in our moral character or behavior—in other words, people who care about us. When formative criticism takes place in the context of personal relationships, it signifies an interest in our moral development, while also highlighting areas for moral improvement. But this can be a tricky balance to strike. The idea that we can both support our friends and family and criticize their behavior is not universally accepted; we hear a lot about "unconditional support," which implies that true support or friendship comes without criticism. I suggest that this is because our scripts around moral criticism are oriented toward opposition, disagreement, and blame, while our scripts around friendship are oriented toward support and acceptance. This makes it difficult to see how we can engage in both: how we can criticize as a friend.

One might grant all of the points made so far and agree that we should critique more often, but doubt that awkwardness explains why we don't. Here it's important to emphasize that there are many reasons someone might not feel comfortable speaking up, approaching a stranger, or getting involved. Fears about physical safety; economic precarity; job (in)security—all of these are real reasons, and the discussion that follows doesn't diminish them one bit. Awkwardness doesn't compete with these—in fact, it can work in tandem with them. If speaking up about racist jokes makes things awkward at work, those in precarious positions, or at risk of discrimination or harassment, are especially vulnerable when advancing moral critique. We often hear words like "fit" thrown around when considering who to hire, promote, or invite for professional opportunities, and making others feel awkward can be taken as evidence that one doesn't "fit." I say this to show that in what follows, awkwardness shouldn't be read as an explanation that diminishes the concerns mentioned above. Instead, it augments them. Our desire to avoid awkwardness is just one of the reasons we self-silence, but it's a significant one. To explain how, let me detour into a different but related phenomenon: the bystander effect.

4.3 The Bystander Effect

In their canonical paper "Bystander Intervention and the Diffusion of Responsibility," Darley and Latané (1968) explored the relationship between the number of bystanders to an emergency and the likelihood that any of those bystanders would help. As the title suggests, they found that as the number of bystanders in the group increased, the percentage of bystanders who helped (in this case, by aiding an experimental confederate faking a seizure) decreased; as group size increased, so, too, did the length of time before someone intervened. Variations on the effect have been found and studied ever since, and the "bystander effect" also makes occasional, attention-grabbing appearances in the media.[7] Indeed, Darley and Latané begin their paper with a description of Kitty Genovese's 1964 murder. At the time, it was widely reported that despite hearing her screams, none of her many neighbors had called the police; as a result of this narrative, the case has become virtually synonymous with bystander inaction. But the facts are more complicated. The oft-repeated claim that no one called the police turns out to be false, a legend growing out of the *New York Times*'s front-page reporting on the crime. In fact, Sophia Farrar, one of Genovese's neighbors, forced open a door to reach her and stayed with her while waiting for emergency responders—a fact the *Times* reported 56 years later, in Farrar's obituary (Roberts 2020).

---

[7] For example, in a 2017 case in Philadelphia, media initially reported that a woman was sexually assaulted on public transportation while other passengers watched and did nothing. The narrative was subsequently called into question, and while it hasn't been definitively debunked, it seems that as in the Kitty Genovese case, the truth is more complicated than initially reported.

4.3.1 Bystander Effects and Ambiguity

The literature on bystander effects has mostly rejected personality-based explanations—it's hard to imagine someone today seriously proposing "alienation" as an explanation, as Darley and Latané did in their original paper. Instead, researchers have shifted to situational explanations, with the bystander effect becoming a staple of the literature on "situationism" (e.g., Doris 2002). One exception is a persistent strand of argument that links the bystander effect to embarrassment—or "embarrassability." According to this explanation, people fail to help because they're afraid of embarrassing themselves. As Miller (1993: 153–154) observes, there's something puzzling about the fact that "many people feel painful awkwardness and embarrassment . . . *doing* certain good deeds." The solution to Miller's puzzlement is that the situation is ambiguous in a way that creates awkwardness: he argues that we feel awkward helping an adult cross the street, but not a child, because our conception of an adult is of someone who does not need help with activities like crossing the street: "Adults who cannot do these things confuse, to our evident distress, the integrity of the categories by which we understand the world." Being confronted with an opportunity to help someone up off the ground "puts us in a quandary of not knowing what to do." Indeed, one group of psychologists have argued that "the really fundamental attribution error" in social psychology involves underestimating the role that people's fear of embarrassment plays in the bystander effect and other apparently situationally determined social behavior (Sabini et al. 2001). Let me explain this argument in a bit more detail, before showing how it links back up to the issue of criticism.

Describing subjects' behavior during the experiment, and their subsequent justifications for it, Darley and Latané write, "It is our impression that non-intervening subjects had not decided not to respond. Rather they were still in a state of indecision and conflict concerning whether to respond or not" (1968: 382). When alone, or with only one other individual, people are much more likely to help, and to do so quickly. But bystanders complicate what would otherwise be a relatively straightforward decision.

The presence of bystanders creates two types of ambiguity. The first concerns who is responsible for helping, or who is going to help. The fact that there are other people around gives the hesitant agent room to think that perhaps someone better-positioned or qualified will step in. Their presence diffuses responsibility for not helping; it licenses hesitation, to wait and see whether someone else *will* help. Second, the presence of bystanders creates normative ambiguity—uncertainty about whether the situation is actually one in which someone *should* help. This can take the form of doubt about whether someone is actually doing anything wrong, or anything that would warrant helping or intervention (a parent saying horrible things to a child in the grocery store is deplorable, but does it merit a stranger's intervention?) or because one might think there is a norm or relevant piece of knowledge of which one is unaware. In another illustration of pluralistic ignorance, people tend to "underestimate the lengths to which other people would go to avoid embarrassment" (Sabini, Siepmann, & Stein 2001: 4),[8] so they imagine that others have a good reason for not intervening—in each bystander's mind, there must be some reason, above and beyond the fear of embarrassment, that explains why no one else is getting involved.

The presence of others creates ambiguity about my role in the situation (am *I* the person to intervene here?) and ambiguity about the norms governing the situation (is this a situation someone *should* intervene in?). This helps make sense of the relationship between the number of bystanders and the strength of the effect: a greater number of people present increases the salience of the fact that no one else is helping, which reinforces the normative ambiguity

---

[8] The authors draw an explicit connection between pluralistic ignorance and fear of embarrassment in a footnote.

(because why would *so many* people choose not to help?) and further diffuses responsibility (because it's distributed among more people).

4.4 Morally Awkward Problems

Ambiguity plays a crucial role in both the bystander case and the self-silencing of moral critique. And it's not just any kind of ambiguity, but the kind that arises when we lack a sense of our role in the situation or a sense of what the norms of the situation involve. In other words, we might say that both the bystander effect and the self-silencing effect are morally awkward problems: they happen because we lack a script for the situation.

In bystander cases, the presence of other people creates ambiguities which lead to inaction. In cases of critique (or lack thereof), ambiguity also plays a role, but the cause isn't the presence of others. Instead, the ambiguity attaches to how we interpret and categorize the normative status of the issue involved: our standing to criticize; the status of the act we're criticizing; and the kind of criticism we're communicating (and not communicating). In the next section, I say more about why this ambiguity arises.

4.4.1 Moral Ambiguity, Moral Awkwardness

The first source of ambiguity is also the most straightforward and familiar: not being confident in one's moral judgment. Perhaps this is because one believes there's a right answer one lacks; alternatively, one might reject the assumption that there's a single correct answer, but still feel unsure about what one ought to do. For example, is it permissible to reprimand someone else's children? Someone might not know where they stand on the situation, either because they don't know what their own commitments and values dictate or because they're not sure they have all the relevant facts. Here, awkwardness isn't (or isn't only) the result of not knowing how someone else expects me to act; it's the result of not knowing how *I* think I should act. As we've seen, scripts don't just tell us what others expect, or what a situation demands: they help us classify and judge events, as well as our own emotions and reactions. If we don't know what we think about an issue, we're susceptible to awkwardness when called to react.

This gives rise to a second, deeper kind of ambiguity involving the status of the norm or issue itself: is this the sort of question about which I ought to intervene? We tend to cordon off some issues—in particular, issues involving food, sex, and family—as playing out within a personal sphere. These aren't "just" questions of personal taste, but they are personal. For example, the norms that govern food choice have historically been fixed by religion, culture, or health; our reasons for avoiding shellfish, for example, or dairy, have been rooted in our identity. Only relatively recently have moral commitments entered the picture in such a way as to vastly expand the range of possible foods we can choose from, making our food choices a matter of both individual choice and global significance—and the sort of thing we might be expected to justify to others. Compare health-related behaviors like fitness or smoking: we've undergone a shift in how we conceptualize many of these issues, moving them from the category of personal to moral in a process of "moralization" (Rozin 1997; Brandt & Rozin 1997). As issues are moralized, the scripts governing how we negotiate them likewise shift, and we can be caught off-guard, or uncertain about the norms that apply, during the transition. There's room here for both genuine ambiguity, issues that are not determinately moral or personal, or that occupy both spheres, and epistemic uncertainty, where there may be a right way to categorize the issue, but we just don't know what it is or how to find it.

Recognizing an issue as moral gives us a starting point for how to approach it, even if we're not sure what the situation demands: we at least recognize that it holds a certain amount of importance, and that we're entitled to an opinion about it, even if others disagree.[9] But when it comes to issues involving food and sustainability, fashion, identity, or politics, we don't even have this much: it's not clear whether the issue is moral, a matter of personal preference, or both. One's consumer behavior is both an expression of individualism and an expression of one's social values; it also has a moral impact. But the norms governing these domains conflict, and it's often unclear which set of norms, and which scripts, we should be following. In cases involving issues like these, we often lack a settled view about their normative status and, correspondingly, what the norms guiding the conversation should be.

It's not surprising that such conflicts arise: for most of our evolutionary history, we interacted with people who shared our norms. In the past, we also had more institutional contexts for critique, through religion and ritual, which provided scripts for giving and responding to moral critique. These institutions clarified the role we played in one another's normative lives—who is responsible for critiquing others, and when and why. In their absence, we're left on our own to navigate a growing menu of options: what to eat, and when, and how often; how to dress; who to socialize with; who to have sex with; who to fantasize about having sex with.

This proliferation of choice has opened up new possibilities for awkwardness, as we face both unscripted issues and choices between the scripts available to us. It's taken place alongside changes in our classification of issues as moral versus social; public versus private. Food, sex, fashion, and consumption—seem like matters

---

[9] This is controversial. I'm trying to remain fairly neutral here about the difference between moral and non-moral issues. There are a number of approaches to distinguishing the two: in terms of the psychological role they play; the conceptual structure of the "oughts" involved; and the content of the various domains. For my purposes, what matters is the recognition that as a descriptive matter, we do sometimes move items between these domains. Readers who are skeptical of any real divide between the moral and social or conventional domains can think of the issue here in terms of our changing attitudes toward private versus public issues.

of personal choice and expression; on the other hand, the choices we make about these issues have far-reaching moral consequences. And while they seem private, increasingly, we make these choices in public. (I say more about the implications of where we negotiate these choices in chapter 6.) Issues like these limn the space between moral and social, sitting uncomfortably on the boundary, and in this sense our uncertainty about how to approach them is well-founded: these are morally awkward issues. They don't fit neatly into the category of moral or social, and this is not just a theoretical wrinkle—it's a practical one. First, the norms around how we discuss personal topics are different from the norms around how we discuss moral issues, so even if we were sure about the right script to use for moral critique (and I don't think we are) we would be left unsure about which script to use on *this* occasion, because we don't know which category this falls into. Second, this leaves us unsure about whether we have the standing to issue criticism. This uncertainty comes partly from not knowing the type of issue involved—my standing to criticize you for a moral transgression might be different from my standing to criticize you for a personal one, in that more people will have the former type of standing than the latter—but it also comes from not being sure of our roles and responsibilities in one another's moral lives.

I've been arguing that in the course of our everyday moral lives, we run into issues that are ambiguous in one or more of the ways described above, and these become morally awkward problems. Either we're unsure how to respond, unsure of our standing to act or issue criticism, or unsure about the status of the issue itself (is it moral, social, or private?). An issue can be ambiguous in one or all of these ways; uncertainty about one can explain or reinforce uncertainty about another. One might wonder, though, whether this is really a new or interesting problem: hasn't uncertainty always been a feature of our moral lives and deliberations? Perhaps, but philosophy tends to characterize it as a passing phenomenon on the way to resolution, a problem faced by individuals trying to fix their beliefs, rather than a predictable and inevitable feature of a changing moral landscape.

4.4.2 Resolvism and Reflection

Even where our classification of an issue is clearly moral, morally awkward problems can arise out of genuine moral ambiguity, the kind involved in deciding whether a particular instance of meat-eating is morally wrong. Throughout this chapter, my examples have focused on food and sustainability. That's because these issues involve empirical facts that are rapidly changing,[10] so our uncertainty about them can be explained in terms other than epistemic access (or lack thereof) to the moral facts. Instead, our uncertainty reflects the unsettled nature of the question itself: is vaping "better" than smoking? Is it wrong to patronize a business that donates money to causes one disagrees with? Can you morally justify vacationing in a state that's passed discriminatory laws? Just as our social scripts may not keep up with emerging technologies, roles, and interactions (like a Zoom wedding), the empirical facts underlying our moral landscape shift in ways that render our existing judgments and principles incomplete.

This points to a potential epistemic benefit of awkwardness: by keeping us from expressing judgment or acting in morally awkward problems, it may prevent us from prematurely reaching a moral consensus on these issues. For example, it's possible that discussion of controversial issues makes people increasingly polarized and entrenched in their opinions.[11] By preventing people from

---

[10] For example, 10 years ago cultivated (aka "lab grown") meat was a novelty, having produced only a single burger at a cost of roughly $330,000 (250,000 GBP). Today, chicken grown from stem cells can be purchased in stores and restaurants in Singapore. By the time this book goes to press, perhaps even more markets will have opened up, and more products will be available.

[11] Lord & Lepper 1979; see also Kelly 2008 for discussion in the context of moral disagreement.

discussing their views about certain issues, awkwardness may keep people relatively epistemically modest about them. This is speculative; I'm suggesting that awkwardness can function interpersonally and socially to buy us time to figure out where we stand (I return to this possibility in chapter 6). And it cuts both ways— if awkwardness prevents premature consensus, it also inhibits the kinds of conversations that would allow us to reach a mature, informed consensus down the line. Thus, while it can be useful as a short-term backstop (a kind of conversational emergency break), it's at best a temporary solution to a problem that's not going anywhere.

The indecision and ambiguity described throughout this chapter so far is very different from the kind typically discussed in the philosophy literature, which involves deliberation, a search for reasons, and most of all, time. While moral philosophy centers on dilemmas like the trolley problem and the difficulties they pose to moral decision-making, we encounter these problems from a spectator's perspective, as a disinterested judge.

Even when the choice is our own, the picture of choice we inherit from philosophy emphasizes time and reflection at the expense of verisimilitude. Arpaly (2003: 20) puts the point vividly:

> Characters in Hollywood movies encounter a lot of car chases. Characters in novels rarely wash their hands or do their laundry. And in the work of moral psychologists, people deliberate and reflect a *lot*. They deliberate, one sometimes feels, whenever they perform an action, and certainly whenever they act for good reasons. They also form beliefs based on reflection, because that is what rational agents do.

If the picture of action we inherit from moral psychology is overly deliberative, it is also overly confident. Harbin (2016: 30) points out that the prevailing moral psychology focuses on the question of "how individual agents become able to form moral judgments and act confidently according to them . . . such accounts have implications for what moral acting morally is understood to *feel like*. Agents may feel confirmed ... when they feel decisive, wholehearted, and in control, and concerned about possibly misguided actions when they feel otherwise." This view, which Harbin calls "resolvism," sees moral action as properly issuing from decisiveness or confidence. In fact, such decisiveness is much rarer in everyday life than resolvism would lead us to believe. Thus, not only does most of our moral action issue from a place of indecision or uncertainty, but we experience this as destabilizing—our lack of moral confidence feels like a departure from what moral action is supposed to feel like. Moral uncertainty is morally awkward.

4.5 Vocalizing Dissent and the Ambiguity of Silence

My discussion of moral critique has focused on dyadic interactions: I critique; you're critiqued. But critique is a bystander problem, too: when we don't vocalize disagreement, we give the impression of assent or weaken the impression of dissent. This risks undermining both the norm being violated—by confusing the question of what our normative expectations are—and accountability to that norm. As we've seen, norms play an important role in creating and maintaining accountability. My belief in the existence of a norm against littering, or in favor of recycling, involves the idea that others hold certain normative expectations. If I have no sense that others disapprove of my (apparently) counternormative actions, my belief about which norms are in effect changes. This is similar to the phenomenon of "moral drift" (Sabini & Silver 1982), in which our failure to express disapproval leads others to think that the action in question is approved of. If that's right, the potential awkwardness of engaging in moral critique may be a cost we risk incurring as individuals to benefit the group.

That's because silence's effects extend beyond the dyad to bystanders and witnesses. As Goldberg (2020: 7) points out, when observing "face-to-face conversations . . . we also typically attend to others' attending to the same speech acts." Goldberg calls this "higher order uptake"—our uptake of others' uptake. Or, in this case, others' lack of uptake. In other words, how are others reacting to what's said? Goldberg is interested in what happens when we reject an assertion without verbally or observably signaling rejection. Typically, audiences are entitled to assume a norm he calls "no silent rejection," which requires us to publicly signal our rejection of an utterance. This allows us to coordinate our position with others, and it also allows others to take silence as a sign of agreement. When rejection is silent, silence no longer plays a useful epistemic role. In particular, self-silencing because of politeness deprives us of a useful tool—the ability to infer assent from silence. Politeness can lead to awkwardness when it leads to uncertainty about what a silence signifies—does the silence mean acceptance, rejection, or some third state (rejection isn't the only kind of uptake failure, after all)? Awkwardness undermines the meaningfulness of silence insofar as it makes silences ambiguous, but the desire to avoid awkwardness also gives people a reason not to observably reject an assertion—especially if they're not sure how others are responding to it.

Staying silent when we reject an assertion diminishes the significance of silence, and degrades our ability to use silence to meaningfully convey agreement, by rendering the meaning of silence ambiguous. Ironically, such silence itself can be awkward, since we no longer know what it means or how to respond to it. I say more about this issue in the next chapter.

4.6 Moral versus Social Motives

Our aversion to awkwardness, and its role in shaping our moral practice, reveals the power of social motives. Philosophers have tended to assume that even if moral reasons don't always trump social pressure, they should—that while there may be practical reasons for caving to social discomfort or pressure, moral obligations and considerations take normative priority. Awkwardness complicates this picture. Social motives wield more power than they're often given credit for, and caving to the social in place of the moral isn't as irrational as it might initially seem.

A growing body of research documents the physical toll of social ostracism, embarrassment, incivility, and microaggressions. For example, Cacioppo and Patrick (2008; see especially chapter 6) report that loneliness and a lack of satisfying social interactions increase our physiological responses to stress, so that not only do people suffer from the social isolation itself, but they're actually worse at responding to and recovering from unrelated stressors. Loneliness is also linked to depression, impaired immune response, increased risk of dementia, and overall mortality risk. In sum, social deprivation is not just psychologically painful, it's physically harmful.[12]

Depriving people of social contact wrongs them. We recognize this most clearly when we consider the wrongs of isolating people and denying them contact in prisons or hospitals. Brownlee (2020a, 2020b) argues for a right to social recognition, and a corresponding obligation to socially acknowledge strangers. But note that our need is not just for contact but for *inclusion* (Baumeister & Leary 1995). And while we recognize the wrong of isolating someone in solitary confinement, we're less often struck by the wrongness of socially ostracizing someone or excluding them from a group—we think of it (when we do) as rude, but not as a grave moral wrong. But that may be a significant mistake: "We are so deeply social that meeting our social needs—for decent human contact, acceptance within a community, companionship, loving relations, and interdependent

---

[12] For a meta-analysis of mortality and loneliness, see Holt-Lunstad et al. 2010. For more on the harms of loneliness, see Brownlee 2020a: 28–29.

care—is *more important than meeting almost every other need we have*" (Brownlee 2020b, emphasis mine).

The fundamental need for social inclusion is worth emphasizing, because it has implications for how we prioritize the social and the moral. We tend to assume that the moral comes prior to the social—if not ontogenically, then in terms of justification. A moral reason can justify antisocial behavior, but the reverse is rarely true. Moreover, we judge those who weigh social acceptance over moral obligation, and often rightly so—we don't give someone a pass for allowing racist jokes to be told in their workplace because it would be awkward to say something about it. But we should be wary of inferring from this point—the observation that awkwardness isn't a pass that allows us to opt out of moral obligations—to the idea that it carries no real normative weight at all.

Norms needn't be perceived as moral in order to exert a strong motivational force; this is one lesson we can draw from the Milgram experiment described at the beginning of the chapter. Milgram is, of course, famous for showing that people would obey experimenters' orders to deliver (what they thought were) painful electric shocks to (what they thought were) fellow experimental subjects. But his own graduate students proved unable to follow his orders to ask people on the subway for their seats. (As anyone who's disappointed their graduate supervisor knows, that's a big deal.) This demonstrates the power of social motivation. There's no moral norm against approaching people on the subway, and it's implausible to think that students believed there was. In bystander cases, not intervening often amounts to violating a moral norm to help. And yet the desire to find and follow the right social norm is sometimes strong enough to get us to do that. This is not entirely surprising when we consider the importance of belonging and fitting in for survival—not just to our evolutionary ancestors, but to us, now.

We don't need a belief in objectivity, or a concept like "moral," or "categorical" to make us cooperate with—or disobey—a researcher.

Our own fear of social isolation (or to put it more positively, our desire for social acceptance) does that for us, and is compatible with a much more parsimonious moral psychology: we internalize norms *qua* norms, not as distinctively moral or social. We experience normative motivation, not distinctively moral versus social types of motivation; moral motivation isn't inherently stronger, and moral norms aren't perceived as intrinsically more motivating—though they might be, depending on the occasion. These are controversial claims, of course, requiring more argument than I can give here. However, recent work in the psychology of norms supports a shift toward a model of normative judgment that treats norm acquisition and internalization—and not *morality*—as the relevant evolutionary adaptation, and which focuses on normativity, rather than moral judgment, as the relevant psychological classification (Kelly & Davis 2018; Kelly 2020; Kelly & Setman 2021; Machery 2012, 2018). Again, this is not the place to settle or even pursue the debate. But as philosophers become increasingly attentive to the costs of social injustice, we might come to better appreciate the wrongs of social exclusion—and the motivational power of social discomfort.

4.7 Conclusion

This chapter has described a fairly straightforward relationship between awkwardness and silence: because we're afraid of making things awkward, we refrain from engaging in difficult moral conversations and reproach. It also leads us to refrain from moral action, as illustrated by the familiar phenomenon of the bystander phenomenon—a phenomenon on which awkwardness offers a new gloss. But as Milgram's subway study illustrates, awkwardness's inhibitory effect extends well beyond the moral domain into our social interactions with others—strangers and friends alike. We're often unsure of how to talk about issues like death, racism, illness, or money; as a result, we end up not talking about them at all. This hurts our relationships, and it hurts us as individuals. It also tells us something about our tools for having difficult conversations. In the moral case, I've suggested that a lot of our uncertainty stems from the genuine ambiguity attending some of these issues. But in other cases, the uncertainty is more basic: we don't know what we're supposed to say, or even think. We don't have very good scripts for discussing illness or death, for example. Sale (2021) points out that the declining role of religion in public life has had a significant impact on how we talk—or don't—about death, since religion historically coordinated our rituals and scripts for dealing with grief. In the absence of such guidance, we struggle to know what to say. When the emotional stakes are so high, we fear getting it wrong, but the stakes are exactly why we ought to talk. Our silence makes lonely experiences lonelier. Making it awkward to discuss death makes it awkward for people to talk about the circumstances of their lives.

In the next chapter, I argue that this interaction between awkwardness and silence contributes to both social and epistemic injustice. I examine the ways in which awkwardness is used to silence certain conversations and marginalize agents and their contributions to knowledge.

5
Awkward Silence

5.1 Introduction: Awkward Silences, Awkward Silencing

Awkwardness and silence are frequent companions: awkwardness discourages and actively shuts down conversations, inhibiting attempts to share and develop conceptual resources. In this chapter, I explore the way awkwardness contributes to silence around topics such as gender, race, and disability; I also illustrate how awkwardness reflects and exacerbates disparities in our access to social scripts.

I begin with some general discussion of the phenomenon of silencing. Making things awkward can be a form of refusal to hear others' contributions, or recognize them for what they are. I also talk about the way awkwardness intersects with scripts around gender to create discursive disadvantages for women. Making it awkward to discuss certain topics can also create the impression that these topics are taboo, since our reasons for not discussing them can be ambiguous between the lack of a script and the existence of a norm against discussing the topic. I conclude by returning to the different roles of shame and awkwardness, and reiterating the importance of distinguishing them: if we mistake awkwardness for shame, we mistakenly take a burden on ourselves as individuals that ought to be distributed socially, and we can form mistaken impressions about taboos. We've already seen how ignorance contributes to defective social norms, by preventing us from recognizing others' actual normative attitudes in ways that could help us change and improve those norms. But not all ignorance is what it seems. In some cases, epistemic resources are available, but awkwardness prevents them from being acknowledged or heard. As it turns out, the remedy for awkward silences is awkward conversation.

Before going any further, let me reiterate a point made in chapter 4: awkwardness is far from the only reason that the injustices discussed here exist, and it's far from the only factor that maintains them. There are many additional reasons why we might remain silent about the examples discussed here: shame (about which I say more at the end of the chapter), physical safety and intimidation, and financial and social precarity, to name just a few. By identifying awkwardness as a contributing factor to the silence around things like sexual harassment, I don't mean to trivialize these issues. If it seems strange and even offensive to talk about issues like racism or sexual harassment in terms of awkwardness, it's because we're used to thinking of awkwardness as a fairly minor irritation. But that's not always the case, and one of the points I hope is becoming clear by now (and which I continue to develop in this chapter) is that awkwardness can be darker and more serious than we often recognize: a weapon, wielded in defense of the status quo.

5.2 Making It Awkward: The Social Construction of Ignorance

Social epistemology recognizes that contrary to the individualistic, atomistic picture of inquiry we inherit from the Cartesian tradition, we don't uptake knowledge in a social vacuum. Nor are all inquirers fungible: our social position and identity influence the epistemic resources accessible to us and our ability to communicate those resources to others. As Fricker (2007) emphasizes in her influential discussion of epistemic injustice, prejudice and bias affect our allocation of credibility—whose testimony is treated as worth hearing, and worth believing—and our access to epistemic resources.[1]

Ignorance is social, too: a "substantive epistemic practice" (Alcoff 2007). One way of constructing and maintaining ignorance involves making it awkward for others to share their experiences. It's not a coincidence that we feel uncomfortable talking about subjects like race, fatness, money, and death. We tend to think of these subjects as inherently uncomfortable when in fact, they're uncomfortable precisely because we lack social scripts to help us talk about them. To paraphrase William James, we don't run from openly discussing our salaries because it's awkward; it's awkward because we run from it. What's needed to render such discussions *less* awkward is open discussion of and engagement with the issues and our attitudes toward them, which in turn lets us develop and learn social scripts for engaging with them. But this is the very thing awkwardness precludes. So, awkwardness reinforces the ignorance perpetuated by the silence around these issues. In this section and the next, I explain one way of thinking about this ignorance: as an instance of hermeneutical injustice. But as we'll see, the problem goes beyond ignorance; in other cases, we have the resources we need, but the problem is communicating and gaining acceptance for them. That problem is the subject of sections 5.4 and 5.5.

By denying people the conceptual resources to make sense of their own experience, and erecting social barriers to the exchange and dissemination of resources, awkwardness inhibits the development of epistemic resources and the exercise of epistemic agency.[2] Awkwardness can also erase knowledge where it previously existed, by preventing us from acknowledging subjects that were once more

---

[1] For discussions of how standpoint influences epistemic privilege, see Anderson 1995 and Wylie 2012; for a discussion of standpoint in terms of epistemic injustice, see Fricker 2007 and Medina 2013.

[2] For discussions of epistemic agency, see Pohlhaus 2020; Catala, Faucher, & Poirer 2021.

openly shared. Discussions of our defecatory habits, for example, were historically treated as important diagnostic information—there's even evidence for a kind of proto-fecal transplantation in ancient Chinese medicine.[3] In more recent history, though, defecation is sequestered (both literally and metaphorically), thus obscuring links between gut function and health—a link that is only now being rediscovered by contemporary wellness culture.

Drawing from the literature on epistemic injustice, we can use the term "hermeneutical gap" to refer to cases where we lack the conceptual resources to understand our experience and communicate it to others. Hermeneutical injustice arises when an agent finds herself unable to find these conceptual resources because of inequalities in our collective epistemic practices. When certain groups or identities are "hermeneutically marginalized," they're denied equal participation "in the practices through which social meanings are generated" (Fricker 2007: 6). It should come as no surprise, then, if the resultant meanings do not adequately represent their experiences.

To use one of Fricker's oft-cited examples, it's not a coincidence that we lacked the concept of workplace sexual harassment for so long, nor is that lack simply the result of our failure to "discover" the phenomenon. Rather, the hermeneutical gap functions as a silencing mechanism: lacking a name for the experience, women were unable to make their experiences known to others, and (Fricker argues) to make sense of it for themselves.[4] I say more about this example below, when I talk about how awkwardness stops us from being heard, and from holding others accountable.

Maintaining hermeneutical gaps is one way awkwardness prevents us from communicating our experiences, thus stifling the development of epistemic resources and harming us as knowers.

---

[3] For an historical overview of attitudes toward defecation, see Inglis 2001; for fecal transplantation, see de Groot et al. 2017.
[4] See Berenstain 2020 for a critique of this claim.

But it's not the only way. When we don't discuss our experiences (whether of bodily functions like defecating, or social harms like harassment), we lose the chance to pool our knowledge. But the harms go further than this: awkwardness alienates us from ourselves, by making us less able to understand our physical and emotional experience; it makes us less sure of ourselves and one another, by denying us the tools we need to communicate them; and it prevents our claims from securing the kind of uptake that confirms their intelligibility and legitimacy.

5.3 Awkwardness, Hermeneutical Gaps, and Epistemic Injustice

The absence of scripts for discussing issues like sexual harassment (or salary gaps, or race, or menopause) can be understood in terms of hermeneutical gaps around these areas of experience. Scripts— and the lack thereof—also influence how we classify both emotional and physical sensations and, in doing so, direct our physical and emotional[5] interactions with the world—and ourselves. This raises the intriguing possibility that awkwardness alienates us not just from others but from our own experiences. When we lack the scripts we need to understand our own inner lives, we become awkward strangers to ourselves. For instance (to borrow an example from Maitra 2018), a new mother's inability to identify her experience as an instance of postpartum depression alienates her from her emotional experience. Once she has the concept *postpartum depression* she is able to identify her feelings, which helps not just in communicating them to others and receiving care—though those things are crucially important—but also in experiencing them as a kind of illness, rather than a personal failing.

---

[5] For a discussion of scripts as categorizing and structuring emotion, see Hochschild 1979, Fehr & Russell 1984, Eickers & Prinz 2020, and Munch-Jurisic 2021.

The scripts available to agents also affect their ability to experience and articulate emotions like anxiety, in ways that might prove more or less destructive: Munch-Jurisic argues that having a script which frames anxiety in medicalized terms inclines us to seek help; a script that treats it as a personal failing might only exacerbate the problem. But we don't and can't come to these frameworks on our own: "social context matters... It is insufficient to coin this problem in individualist terms. It is not a form of mere conceptual insufficiency... but a form of *deprivation*. We make sense of the world and our experiences with the mental and emotional resources we draw from the world around us" (Munch-Jurisic 2021: 13595).

Awkwardness deprives us of the kind of social support we get by sharing our experiences in conversation with others. This lack of conversation, in turn, further deprives us of the opportunity to develop the conceptual resources that would make such conversations less awkward. Fricker argues that historically, feminist consciousness-raising groups have played a crucial role in this process, allowing women to share their "scantly understood, barely articulate experiences," which allows the coining of terms like "sexual harassment," but also a better understanding of experiences like postpartum depression (2007: 148–149). Consider this passage from Susan Brownmiller's memoirs, in which a woman describes learning the term "postpartum depression": "I realized that what I'd been blaming myself for, and what my husband had blamed me for, wasn't a personal deficiency. It was a combination of physiological things and a real social thing, isolation" (Fricker 2007: 149).

More recently, Hardy and Kukla describe the way online communities and discussion boards help women navigate the "distinctively hard-to-articulate experience" of miscarriage, which "resists easy assimilation into a widely recognizable narrative" (2015: 109). Developing hermeneutical resources can require difficult conversations, and groups like these function as a place where discomfort is built into the script: it's expected that the conversations will involve experiences that are difficult to describe and share. We may even come to view the ensuing discomfort as a sign of progress rather than as a problem to be overcome. As Harbin (2016: 79) notes, "Experiences of unease, discomfort, and fear were thus not merely accidental features of participation in such groups but expected, meaningful components of efforts to confront internalized 'oppression.'"

The discomfort and disorientation we experience when discussing certain topics—sexual harassment, miscarriage, female orgasm[6]—are informative, alerting us to areas where our scripts are insufficient. And expecting the discomfort involved in discussing these topics prepares us to confront it. That might seem like an odd claim, because elsewhere (for example, in chapter 4's discussion of moral criticism) I've suggested that expecting something to be awkward is a deterrent to confronting it. But as Harbin notes, in these contexts, discomfort is framed as a "meaningful" consequence of resisting oppression, which changes the significance of our feelings: they're a shared part of the work involved in changing social norms, not an alienating sign of social misattunement or a warning of impending ostracism. Here, discomfort highlights the extent to which we've internalized the very social norms and expectations we want to resist, drawing our attention to the contingency of the expectations to which we hold ourselves.

Willingness to speak is not enough, though: open discussion also requires a willingness to listen. What's special about the kinds of environments described here is the commitment to receptivity that's built into the situation, even if that receptivity means discomfort for speakers or audiences. That's partly a consequence of the lack of hermeneutical resources available to members of these groups—when we know we'll face difficulty communicating certain experiences, we enter into the task prepared for a challenge.

---

[6] On the study of female orgasm as an example of manufactured ignorance, see Tuana 2004.

Fricker's discussion of hermeneutical injustice shows that sometimes awkwardness happens because we lack the concepts we need. But awkwardness also happens when the words we have are attached to ambiguous or evolving meanings, such that we're unsure what they would actually commit us to saying. In this case, the problem isn't a hermeneutical gap per se—it's an ambiguity in the normative meanings attached to certain terms or concepts. For example, consider "fat," a term once widely viewed as pejorative, but currently in the process of being reclaimed as a neutral description, if not a point of pride (Manne 2024). The stigma surrounding fatness has lent the term a pejorative air, leading both media and personal discussions to opt for what seems like a more neutral alternative: obese. But as we've taken a more critical stance toward the harms of fatphobia, writers have pointed out that the language of obesity is stigmatizing in its own way; talk of the "obesity epidemic" associates fat bodies with disease and contagion, and many writers and activists now urge us to embrace the language of fat and fatness (LeBesco 2010). As the meaning of "fat" has shifted, we're unsure which meanings our audience associates with a term. We might even be unsure what our own norms and values around the issue are, as we become aware of the extent to which they're conditioned by the diet culture that surrounds us.[7] As a result of this uncertainty, and the ambiguous normative connotations of the term, talking about fatness becomes awkward. Writers and educators can avert potential awkwardness by flagging and explaining their use of the term "fat." In this case, we don't evolve a new hermeneutical resource; we confront the confusion surrounding the resources we have, and acknowledge the attendant discomfort.

Making the expectation of discomfort explicit also means that we interpret others' hesitation and silence as reflections of the difficulty of the topics being discussed, not as rejections of our own attempts at talking about them. This is important, since as we've

---

[7] See Manne 2024 for a discussion of diet culture and fatphobia.

seen in the previous chapter, silence creates ambiguity, and can be interpreted as a form of rejection. In the next section, I talk more about the interplay between awkwardness, silence, and silencing.

5.4 The Weaponization of Awkwardness

So far, I've discussed the idea that hermeneutical gaps are one reason why subjects are awkward to discuss; another is our uncertainty about the normative commitments of our language. But the question remains, how does communication itself break down into awkward silence? One way involves simply avoiding the discussion entirely. But another involves the response our claims receive (or don't receive) from others. If we must play along with certain scripts in order to make ourselves understood, conformity to a script becomes a condition of intelligibility. And refusing to grant intelligibility is one way of resisting attempts to shift our scripts. In this section, I look more closely at how our scripts around gender, in particular, can doom our speech acts to failure, forcing us into awkward silence.

Kukla (2014: 445) describes the case of Celia, a floor manager at a factory, whose job is to issue orders to her employees—almost all of whom are male. Celia is viewed as a "bitch" by the other workers, not because they're overtly and explicitly sexist, but because scripts around women and power prevent the workers from hearing Celia's speech as orders, rather than as requests.[8]

As the example shows, our ability to perform a particular speech act depends on the other scripts at work in our environment: if others can't or won't uptake my speech act as an order, or a complaint, or an objection, my attempt to order, complain, or object is thwarted. But in other cases, the failure is more general: a refusal by

---

[8] I've adapted the wording here to put the point in terms of scripts; Kukla describes the case in terms of conventions and social narratives.

audiences to uptake a certain type of claim or to hear a certain kind of speaker.

Pohlhaus (2012: 729) describes "willful hermeneutical ignorance" as arising from a refusal to acknowledge others' experiences, which skews our hermeneutical resources in favor of a certain perspective. Pohlhaus explains: "when a group with material power is vested in ignoring certain parts of the world, they can . . . maintain their ignorance by refusing to recognize and by actively undermining any newly generated epistemic resource that attends to those parts of the world they are vested in ignoring." Awkwardness is one way this refusal manifests. In these cases, awkward silence is better described as awkward silenc*ing*: occasions where an utterance is made, or a topic raised, but its status is left uncertain, because it's unclear what kind of uptake, if any, it has received.

Sometimes refusal to uptake speech takes the form of straightforward, explicit rejection of the speaker's claims. But it can also take a subtler form: questions, requests for more information, the expression of doubt.

This subtler form is where we start to see the pernicious and undermining effects of awkwardness. For example, consider a graduate student attempting to report her peers for making sexist comments about women's philosophical abilities. Her department chair might accept the complaint or he might reject it; in between is a range of skeptical responses that leave the issue unsettled—repeated requests for clarification, asking the student what she would have him do, and so on. This response is awkward both because it creates confusion about what, exactly, is happening (is he accepting her complaint?) and because it puts the student in the middle of two conflicting scripts—she is supposed to defer to her supervisor; she doesn't want to be cast as "pushy," but it's unclear how to navigate this now-puzzling interaction. Like Celia in our earlier example, the graduate student's ability to make a complaint is undermined by her audience's unwillingness to hear it, leaving her in an awkward limbo.

Garber (2017) argues that awkwardness, and discomfort more generally, is often "weaponized" by abusers: "men accused of predation, it has now become painfully clear, have in their own way used these crushing social pressures as weapons," not only by cautioning women to stay silent lest they "make a scene," but by counting on audiences' unwillingness to receive women's complaints, because dealing with harassment—and dealing with harassers, who might be one's coworkers or friends—is awkward. Garber describes the way women who report workplace harassment are often frozen out or met with silence: "no one knocked on my door," one woman quoted in the piece reports, "no one spoke to me much at all" (Garber 2017). Decades after introducing the concept "sexual harassment," the hermeneutical gap is closed. But it's not enough to have the language to voice complaints of harassment—change and progress requires a receptive audience to uptake them.

The complex set of assumptions that background any given exchange renders our speech subject to failure or misinterpretation for any number of reasons, and along any number of lines, as Kukla (2014: 440–441) observes:

> I decide whether someone is using her words to order, request, inquire, propose, report, and so on by interpreting her as deploying a wide array of explicit and implicit conventions governing context, tone, gesture, conversational flow, and more. Sometimes . . . I interpret the force of another's speech as effortlessly as I do its content. . . . At other times . . . I might struggle hard to decide how to situate and interpret the force of a speech act amid the web of conventions, rituals, and circumstantial clues that make up its context.

As we've already seen, miscommunications can be more or less innocent, and failures of uptake can take a variety of forms, from genuine confusion to willful ignorance to manipulative, even spiteful refusal.

When speech doesn't receive the desired or intended uptake, it's not always clear what the reason is, leaving speakers uncertain where the fault (if any) lies. This can deter others from making similar claims. One of Garber's subjects recounts that no one at her workplace spoke to her about her harassment complaint at the time, years later, another woman acknowledged having known about it: when she was later harassed by the same editor, "she didn't bother telling anyone" (Wildman 2017).

5.5 Expression, Awkwardness, and Discursive Disadvantage

As the discussion so far shows, our ability to communicate feelings, complaints, or emotions isn't entirely up to speakers; it requires " the collaboration of interpreters," in determining the meaning of expressions of emotions or intent. For example, "my reluctance to do something may be read as a form of stubbornness in any situation where people are unwilling to understand the reasons for my nonparticipation" (Campbell 1994: 51). We depend on others to receive our expressions and grant them meaning. This leaves us vulnerable to misinterpretation. In Campbell's example, stereotypes of women as overly emotional lead the speaker's reasons for refusal to be overlooked; she's interpreted as irrationally stubborn. Misinterpretations are sometimes due to aspects of an agent's identity; they can also be reactions to an agent's style of communication: her emotionality, physicality, speech, or vocabulary. In this section I discuss awkward silencing based on an agent's identity or communicative style.

What we might call "expressive awkwardness" emerges when listeners are unwilling to accept or understand speakers' modes of self-expression. In cases of expressive awkwardness, agents are treated as awkward, and/or viewed as the cause of awkwardness, in virtue of others' inability or refusal to engage with their communicative styles. For example, Catala, Faucher, and Poirier (2021: 9) note:

> Autistic persons often communicate through the use of (neuro) atypical verbal and nonverbal expressive styles, for example through echolalia (repeating words or a sentence uttered by others) or motor stereotypies (repeated movements or gestures)... these communicative attempts are often mistakenly perceived as meaningless, when in fact they are often used by autistic persons to express important aspects of their experiences, like an emotion (e.g., excitement or anxiety), a position (e.g., agreement), or an interpretation of their situation.

The authors emphasize the epistemic injustice involved here: autistic speakers' contributions receive less credibility, which is a form of testimonial injustice; insofar as it prevents them from contributing their knowledge and experiences to our epistemic resources, it also contributes to hermeneutical injustice. Indeed, this seems like a case of what Medina (2017: 46) describes as "performatively produced" hermeneutical injustice—cases in which subjects are seen as "unintelligible or less intelligible... not because of the words they use but because of their communicative performance or expressive style."[9] Our failure to uptake these communicative attempts can lead to awkwardness. Worse, our reaction to "dissonant or eccentric voices" (46) and communicative styles often involves labeling (and dismissing) the speakers as awkward.[10] This judgment diminishes our willingness to genuinely engage and listen, which in turn feeds back into the judgment that the fault lies in the speaker.

---

[9] To be clear, Medina isn't referring to neurodivergence specifically but to various aspects of performance, including accents, word choice, and communicative style.

[10] For example, see Grossman 2015 and White, Hillier, Frye, & Makrez 2019 on neurotypical students' attitudes toward interactions with their neurodivergent peers.

But whether or not an expressive style is intelligible depends in large part on the communicative and expressive norms in play in a context—in other words, on the scripts governing communication in those contexts. Observing interactions between autistic people, researchers find "a well-developed set of social norms for handling and interpreting the very set of behaviors that [other researchers] identify as potentially misconstrued by non-autistic people" (Heasman & Gillespie 2019: 26). In other words, the awkwardness arises not because of an expressive style per se, but because that mode of expression falls outside the competence of the non-autistic actor. This highlights two things: first, reducing awkwardness needn't require changing expressive styles; it might be enough to broaden our interpretive resources. Second, doing this might involve attending to the very individuals or experiences that are at risk of being excluded as unintelligible or left out of interactions on the basis of expressive awkwardness. If the question of how to understand social cues from autistic people is an epistemic problem, it's partly because we've excluded autistic experience from our social understanding: "What counts as signaling social interest will depend on whether one is an autistic actor or a neurotypical observer. A more interactional intervention would be re-educating neurotypical people through learning from autistic social appraisal, so as to diversify neurotypical understanding of autistic social behavior" (Heasman & Gillespie 2019: 26).

In previous chapters, I've emphasized the harm of social exclusion. It leads to loneliness, it has significant negative effects on well-being, and it limits the stock of social resources one is able to access—including, but not limited to, social scripts. In that last respect, social exclusion is also self-reinforcing: the less one is included, the more awkward one becomes. And it's tempting to think of the harm there as accruing only to the excluded individual, but as the discussion above shows, marginalized groups develop social resources of their own, and excluding them from interactions and social scripts results in an impoverished set of epistemic resources for everyone.

In cases of neurodivergence, speakers may not have the option to alter their expressive style or presentation. But in other cases, the need to exert such control in order to make oneself understood imposes an extra burden, as speakers work to make their affect and style acceptable—or opt to withhold expression altogether, suppressing emotion or even speech. Bailey (2018: 100) uses the term "affective smothering" to describe "a type of self-tone-policing that happens when a speaker recognizes that the audience lacks either the empathy or the affective competence to make sense of her anger." The author John Hendrickson describes the self-imposed silence he experiences as a stutterer: "Nearly every decision in my life has been shaped by my struggle to speak. I've slinked away to the men's room rather than say my name during introductions. I've stayed home to eat silently in front of the TV rather than struggle for a brief moment at a restaurant." Hendrickson is acutely aware of the effect his speech has on audiences: "an awkward exchange between two people affects not just the person being awkward, but the person forced to deal with said awkwardness. A stutterer may enter a room full of 'normal' people and temporarily pass as a fellow 'normal,' but the moment they open their mouth—the second that jagged speech hits another set of eyes and ears—it's over" (Hendrickson 2023).

As we saw in section 5.4, silencing sometimes involves explicit dismissal, or misunderstanding, in which case the remedy seems to require pushing the point: restating a claim, insisting on a point, demanding recognition. This is another place where social scripts can hold us back. For example, women are expected to be caring, supportive, and giving, not confrontational and demanding: "women are supposed to minister to others, rather than solicit moral concern and attention on their own behalf" (Manne 2018: 282). These very public dismissals contribute to social scripts that condition women to withhold complaints (regardless of how justified they might be), and to prioritize others' comfort over our own. Pressing claims that make others feel uncomfortable—and that make situations awkward—is doubly difficult: it forces women to articulate our complaints forcefully (despite the fact that doing so makes us liable to be dismissed as "shrill," as Manne notes),[11] and it puts us in a position where we're forced to choose between articulating our concerns and managing others' social discomfort.

When a situation requires us to push a point that makes others uncomfortable, it challenges scripts that cast women as emotional "givers"; departing from this script, we may feel awkward, or bad for making others feel awkward. Doing so doubly violates the obligations these scripts assign to women: to "give feminine-coded services" such as kindness, admiration, and comfort, and to refrain from "taking masculine-coded goods" such as power, prestige, and face (Manne 2018: 130). Women are therefore put in a position where speaking about the issues that most directly impact them (materially and emotionally) incurs emotional as well as epistemic labor: we have to figure out how to have the conversation and then clean up the resulting social mess.[12]

Awkward situations thus put women at a double discursive disadvantage. Our scripts prescribe deferential behavior and social repair—women's role is to facilitate social interactions, smooth out social discomfort, and make others comfortable. We see this trope in action when we're told women have greater social and emotional intelligence, superior social skills, are more comfortable with emotions, and so on. Where conversations get uncomfortable, it's women's work to repair them. On the other hand, we have a dearth of social scripts for conversations about salary gaps, periods, postpartum bodies, and so on. As a result, those conversations are bound to get awkward. And the threat of discomfort—including,

---

[11] For example, see Manne's discussion of the 2016 election coverage: critics who pointed out the role of misogyny in Clinton's defeat were dismissed and discredited, despite the ample evidence and expertise on their side.
[12] See Hochschild 1979 for more on emotional labor.

but not limited to, awkwardness—can make us discount others' testimony or assertions (lest they force us to confront uncomfortable truths), or make us reluctant to engage with certain speakers in the first place.

All of this means that in addition to navigating unclear social scripts, speakers may be tasked with anticipating and managing others' emotions, and their own, both because of social expectations and in order to secure uptake for their claims. Recall how Garber's subjects were met with awkward silence when they tried to report harassment; one woman even reports being told to tell her harasser (who was also the editor in chief of the magazine she worked at) that she'd been the one to complain, lest he learn about it from someone else in the office. Because that might make things awkward.

Of course, women are not the only ones disadvantaged by awkward silencing. Goffman describes how individuals with visible disabilities develop strategies for calling attention to and acknowledging them, as an "ice-breaking" strategy to avert potential awkwardness. The point is echoed by experiments suggesting that interactions between disabled and nondisabled participants were viewed more positively when the disabled person acknowledged and drew attention to their disability early on. The acknowledgment serves as a social cue to the nondisabled party, helping them navigate the interaction and relieving their awkward feelings (Hebl, Tickle, & Heatherton 2000). But note that this relief is achieved through largely via the emotional labor of the disabled person (Scully 2010). Disabled people may also feel pressure to avoid showing certain emotions, lest they make the situation uncomfortable for others. Cahill and Eggleston describe

> the emotional dilemmas that wheelchair users face when in public places: they must attempt to remain poised and good-humored in frustrating and potentially embarrassing circumstances without thereby increasing others' already considerable discomfort

at those circumstances. In public places they often have the double duty of managing both their own and others' emotions. (1994: 303)

Here again, the emotional work of managing others' comfort while masking their own frustrations falls disproportionately on one party to the interaction.

5.6 Scripts, Power, and Privilege

A lack of social relationships limits our access to scripts and social roles, making us even more vulnerable to awkwardness. This is partly because there are certain topics one can discuss without fear of awkwardness in the context of a close friendship, but not in other social contexts. In these cases, awkwardness—or a lack thereof—can function as a diagnostic test of a relationship: is it awkward for us to watch a movie with sex scenes? Is it awkward to discuss feces or periods? Questions like these help calibrate degrees of intimacy; if two friends answer them differently, things can get awkward. Bodily functions might seem like a relatively trivial example compared to issues like misogyny, racism, and sexual harassment. But an inability to discuss bodily functions can be alienating, too, and my point is that when our social relationships are limited by awkwardness, so, too, is our ability to communicate our experiences. This in turn alienates us, not just from others, but from ourselves.

Consider the example of perimenopause. Many people who menstruate are unprepared for the sudden and dramatic hormonal changes that can predate the onset of menopause by up to 10 years; menopause itself remains a relatively understudied phenomenon. Those experiencing it are often left to navigate conflicting medical advice on their own, a process made even more difficult by the awkwardness of discussing periods, sex, and other bodily functions. In cases like these, friendships are one source of information and support, but they serve the additional function of helping us calibrate our expectations for how to discuss these issues and with whom. In the absence of such friendships, we don't need to draw on the concept of hermeneutical injustice to explain why we feel alienated from our own experiences—the gap in resources is not (or not only) hermeneutical, but social.

Knowing the right script for an occasion is, in many cases, a kind of privileged access; when we place these scripts off-limits to certain groups, we make it more awkward for them to participate in those occasions. We also deprive them of social information and skills, which require practice: knowing how to "read" a performance in a given context can be a matter of correctly interpreting subtle clues, like the meaning of silence, or a sullen glare. When the excluded person does attempt to participate, then, they're out of practice and hence more prone to awkwardness, which in turn can lead us to reject their contributions based on their expressive form, viewing them as inadequate or ill-formed. And this can lead to what Dotson (2011) calls "contributory injustice": the inability to share epistemic resources or to have one's epistemic contributions taken up.

The process isn't necessarily intentional. For example, a professor might not intend to limit students' access to her office hours, but for those who don't know what office hours are for, or how to use them—who don't, in other words, know the "office hours script"—the potential awkwardness of attending might act as a deterrent. In turn, the professor is deprived of their questions and contributions, and left with a skewed perspective on her students' experience of the semester.

Limiting someone's opportunity to contribute to our shared epistemic resources also limits their exercise of epistemic agency (Pohlhaus 2020). Part of what it is to exercise epistemic agency is to be able to effect epistemic change; excluding or dismissing someone prevents them from doing that. In the discussion of expressive awkwardness above, I mentioned the possibility of learning new modes of communication and new social norms by observing interactions between people with different expressive styles—autistic people, for example. Doing so doesn't just add to our stock of epistemic resources, it augments others' epistemic agency by allowing us to hear and uptake their testimony, experiences, and knowledge.

Frye (1983) describes a case where a woman customer becomes angry with a mechanic who won't stop messing with her carefully adjusted carburetor; the mechanic reacts by dismissing the customer as a "crazy bitch." Frye uses the example to illustrate how a woman's anger is denied uptake, despite her very real grounds for indignation (apparently, a carburetor is finicky and takes a lot of work to properly adjust). In this case, the dismissal of her righteous anger stems in part from the refusal to grant her epistemic agency. Since she couldn't possibly know more about cars than the mechanic, her anger must be irrational.

Another way that awkwardness reinforces existing inequities has to do with how and when we proffer scripts to others—or withhold them. When we respond to someone as though they're unintelligible, we are refusing to acknowledge the script they're proposing; we either force them into our own chosen script (she is a crazy bitch, or pushy; he is autistic, his vocalizations are meaningless) or we leave them out in the hermeneutical cold, awkwardly stranded without a script to follow. Earlier, I mentioned the possibility that awkwardness is alienating: when others shift the script on us, we're forced to either abandon our original meanings or identities and play along, or stubbornly insist on them, and make things awkward. In other words, we're forced to choose between alienation from our identity, or alienation from others. A "crazy bitch" is intelligible to the sexist mechanic; a righteously angry skilled amateur mechanic—who is also a woman—is not. And while in this case, alienation from others may not seem like such a bad outcome, we often depend on social inclusion not only for our general well-being, but for our basic safety.

In the thick of awkwardness, we may accept whichever script we see handy; this puts us at a disadvantage if we're not in a position to negotiate—we may be forced to accept unjust or harmful terms. This is a consequence of the rather obvious fact that not all scripts are equally good, fair, kind, or even useful. In an awkward situation, the person who sets the terms of the encounter enjoys an advantage, and someone who's unfamiliar with the situation and the appropriate scripts is at a corresponding disadvantage—escaping awkwardness requires them to accept some sort of script, but they may have little to say about which that ends up being.

This is one reason we sometimes play along with scripts in the moment and then later explain the situation in other terms. And when someone does that, it's not because they changed their mind, or were too "afraid," or "embarrassed," it's because enacting a social script is a joint enterprise, and the "this guy is a creep" script may simply not be available at that moment to that person. There are two lessons here: first, not all routes out of awkwardness are equal. Second, power doesn't just manifest in the creation of awkwardness but in its resolution, too.

In her work on complaints, Ahmed (2019: 521) describes how a bystander to harassment pressures the "complainer" to reconceptualize the interaction: "The staff member in advising her ... by leaning in this way, positions himself with the harasser, treating the verbal onslaught as joke, something she should take; something she should be willing to take." Here we see the pressure to adopt a certain script retroactively—her experience at the time notwithstanding, she should see it now as the staff member understands it, a joke. We also see the significance of viewing the interaction through the lens of a given script: a jocular exchange between colleagues, rather than harassment. It hardly needs saying that to reject the script others are pushing, in circumstances like these, is not just awkward but extremely socially costly. But I'll say it anyway: pushing back on a social script, by refusing to play along, or insisting on an alternative, comes at a significant cost.

In chapter 2, I suggested that the phenomenological aspects of awkwardness could be understood in terms of our attunement—or lack thereof—to others. Ahmed uses the term "mood work" to describe a process by which the experience of misattunement becomes a technique for modifying behavior. In mood work, the significance of misattunement lies not just in being out of sync but in the sudden *loss* of attunement. To be attuned is to share "an affective valuation"; when this is disrupted, we find ourselves suddenly out of sync, physically or affectively or both. Those perceived as responsible for this misattunement are seen as "obstacles ... in the way not only of attunement, but all that it promises: life, connection, empathy, and so on" (2014: 20). If this sounds like a burden, it is: the disruption of attunement, and the individual deemed responsible, become a source of tension. Restoring attunement becomes their job, which requires managing others' moods and emotions as well as one's own. Misattunement, and the mood work that it creates, can function as a form of punishment or pressure to bring oneself back into alignment with the group. It's not just the wrong actions, or utterances, that make for awkwardness, but the wrong stance: declining to share or endorse someone else's evaluative or affective orientation can be a way of alienating them from us.

5.7 Awkwardness as Activism?

But it's not all bad. Making things awkward can be a way of highlighting bad behavior, and of "unofficially" holding someone accountable for a transgression when we have relatively little institutional power or means to do so. For example, suppose someone attempts to make a sexist joke at a work event, and instead of laughing, everyone remains silent: the situation becomes awkward. This is one way to reject the speaker's effort to make a sexist joke: with awkward silence. It's not ideal; it suffers from the ambiguity discussed in chapter 4, since it's not always clear what silence signifies. Suppose that instead, when the joke is made, a colleague pretends to be confused, and asks for explanation, continuing the questions even as the would-be joker becomes flustered. This is awkward, too, but in a more pointed way: actively making the transgressor feel awkward is a way of drawing attention to, and punishing, the transgression.

For those in a relatively disempowered position, such awkward silence can be a way of resisting racist or sexist speech without making explicit accusations of racism or sexism, accusations that can be costly. It's a way of refusing to assent to misogynistic humor without explicitly refusing to assent.

But in other situations, this tactic can be deployed to undermine accountability. Making things awkward can be a way of rejecting others' attempts at communication, a way of refusing to hear their complaints or understand their attempts to hold others accountable. For example, if a woman attempting to report a colleague's harassment is forced to recount the jokes he told in a meeting with her superior, she may feel awkward repeating his words; a student attempting to report a professor's microaggressions may have to recount and explain why these are incidents of racism. Above, I outlined a situation where a student's attempted complaint was met with questions and confusion rather than support (or outright rejection), leaving her feeling unclear as to how it had been received—in other words, awkward.

We've seen that awkward silence can take several forms: one form involves actual, literal, silence, which is ambiguous, depriving audiences of the cues needed to coordinate on a script. Another form is not giving uptake, so that it's unclear what, if anything, has been communicated. Watching others' assertions fail to get uptake also has a silencing effect on potential future speakers.

Awkward silences accumulate to create silence around certain subjects. When we reject someone's claims or otherwise fail to uptake them, we send a signal to observers that this topic is not one to bring up. And we forego the opportunity to create a script to accommodate the issue, thereby keeping things awkward. But this awkwardness can also be confused for the existence of a taboo. And our awkward feelings can also be confused for shame. In the final section, I discuss the relationship between shame, awkwardness, and taboo.

5.8 Awkwardness, Shame, and Taboo

In practice, taboos and awkwardness can function similarly: an awkward topic can feel like it's taboo, since we feel unable to address it or raise it. But the causes are importantly different, as are the remedies. In the case of a taboo, what stops discussion is the existence of a norm against talking about the topic—a norm that we're aware of (hence our reluctance to broach the topic). In the case of awkwardness, the issue is not that we *know* we shouldn't broach the topic, but uncertainty about whether or how to broach it. Importantly, many taboos are surrounded with norms about how to react to violations: with displays of shame and embarrassment, perhaps, or rituals that perform a repair, apology, or amends. This is not the case with awkwardness, as we've seen in earlier chapters. But it can be hard to disentangle these in practice, because simply observing that a topic isn't discussed doesn't tell us why this is. The impression that a subject is taboo tends to insulate itself against refutation, since it discourages others from raising the subject and thereby correcting the impression. While there's a difference between having a norm that tells us not to discuss a subject because it's shameful or taboo and lacking a script that would allow us to discuss something, in practice, this difference can be hard to detect.

But if "merely" awkward topics can be mistaken for taboo, the relationship also goes the other way: the existence of a taboo can also function to make things awkward, by preventing us from developing the scripts we need to discuss or acknowledge it more widely. For example, in many cultures, menstruation is seen as shameful and is subject to various rites and rituals. But while these attitudes shape norms by which to navigate the experience of menstruation—thereby making it not awkward but taboo—they also confine the acknowledgment of menstruation to certain contexts, outside of which discussing it becomes awkward. A similar point applies to discussion of such issues as postpartum incontinence, breastfeeding, miscarriage, money issues, and so on. In many cases, our normative attitudes surrounding these issues have evolved, so that we no longer regard them as off-limits for discussion, and might even endorse the idea of openly discussing them. However, the fact that they've been considered taboo for so long means that our conceptual resources and scripts lag behind the progression of our attitudes. One might worry that a world in which we freely and openly discuss issues like this with everyone—colleagues, parents, strangers—sounds, horribly invasive. I don't disagree, and I'll address this issue in chapter 6.

One might object that awkwardness is the wrong characterization of the issue here: we don't feel awkward talking about periods, or sexual harassment; we feel shame. In this final section, I take up the question of how shame relates to awkwardness, both to address this concern and to show how understanding awkwardness's role has practical implications—implications we'll continue to explore in the next and final chapter. I won't defend a particular view of shame; while there are various theories of shame and the normative weight we should give it, for my purposes here, what matters is that the distinction between shame and feeling awkward, and that's what I focus on here.

As we saw in chapter 2, shame and awkwardness differ in terms of their phenomenology, roles, and onset. Shame is self-directed and evaluative, and often comes up in retrospect, when one looks back on an event or behavior. Awkwardness is situationally oriented, focusing attention on behavior (or lack thereof), and happens "in the moment." One can't be simultaneously struck by awkwardness and shame—the feelings are too overwhelming to coexist. But shame often follows awkwardness; we feel ashamed of our awkward behavior, especially in recollecting it. That's because shame involves self-evaluation, the sense that we've failed to live up to a standard.[13] If an awkward situation makes us feel shame, it's because it seems to reveal something bigger, more global, about who we are. We feel embarrassed by an accidental belch, but we feel ashamed of our bodies. Moments of awkwardness can make us feel somehow "wrong" or "misfit," and we can view our inability to enact a social script as a reflection on us—that we have failed, or fallen short, or are somehow socially inept or defective.

Like awkwardness, shame is closely linked to silence; lacking a script for how to engage with a subject may lead us to think it's something we shouldn't discuss. More generally, as in our previous discussion of taboos, the fact that a topic is awkward to discuss can make us think there's something shameful about it. Just as scripts become normative, the absence of scripts can become normative, too: we take it to signal something about the social acceptability of an issue, or even of a kind of person. In chapter 3, I argued that our desire for inclusion can lead us to accept roles we'd prefer to reject, because the failure to be "castable" in a script marks one as an outsider. One needn't endorse the available social roles in order to find social exclusion unpleasant, and its looming threat explains why we sometimes find ourselves enacting roles whose normative implications we reject.

"False shame" occurs when we feel ashamed of that which is not shameful.[14] One might reject the idea that women of a certain age should be married and have children, and still feel shame over one's single childlessness at a family gathering. One might shun status

---

[13] As Maibom (2010: 569) puts it, "nearly everyone" agrees on this point, though they disagree on what the relevant standards are and whether to think of the response in terms of self-esteem, self-respect, injury, threat, or diminishment.

[14] Or, to put it in more agent-centered terms: the agent who feels false shame is responding to a norm she does not endorse. For a discussion and critique of the idea of "false shame," see Thomason 2015.

signifiers like a certain kind of car or watch, but still feel shame pulling up at the college reunion in a rusty old beater.

One response is that this kind of shame is irrational.[15] But another response is that this kind of shame is neither mistaken nor irrational but a sign of moral maturity. Calhoun (2004) distinguishes two senses in which we might give weight to an opinion. There's epistemic weight, which involves thinking the opinion is true, rational, or justified—giving it a positive epistemic appraisal. Practical weight, on the other hand, requires no such positive appraisal. What it does require is seeing it "as issuing from those who are to be taken seriously because they are co-participants with us in some shared social practice," and "recognizing that the shamer's opinion expresses a *representative viewpoint* within that practice." We don't have to endorse that viewpoint to be affected by it; indeed, as Calhoun points out, there's a danger in assuming that we are only affected by criticisms we endorse. Rejecting the viewpoint doesn't make us any less vulnerable to it. An agent who feels shame based on others' outlooks "signals their capacity to take seriously fellow participants in their social world . . . to give their opinions 'weight.'" (Calhoun 2004: 138). We may or may not share evaluative commitments or frameworks with others around us; often, we find ourselves thrown together because we share something else—a project, a career choice, a location. These are enough to force us into practical coordination and cooperation, at least to a sufficient extent that we are vulnerable to others' critiques, and not irrational for feeling their weight.

Similar worries arise about awkwardness and social discomfort more generally: why should these affect us when we reject the general evaluative stance from which they issue? For example, if we believe that it should be socially acceptable to discuss money, it's unclear why we would be bothered by the awkwardness of actually

---

[15] See Deigh 1983 and Taylor 1985. See Maibom 2010 for an overview and taxonomy of philosophical accounts of shame.

initiating such a discussion. Alternatively, we might reject or lack regard for a certain individual or their viewpoint—in that case, why should we be susceptible to concerns about making things awkward for them? Part of the reason, of course, is that awkwardness isn't contained, and if someone feels awkward, that awkwardness may spread to us as well: unlike shame, awkwardness is a social phenomenon. But a less self-interested reason is that we're concerned for others, and we don't want them to feel awkward.

The response here runs parallel to the discussion of shame above: we're affected by the awkwardness of a situation even if we don't "endorse" it, because as social creatures we're susceptible to the evaluative standards of others. We describe (and disparage) some people as "shameless"; less-so, "awkward-less." Many of us do feel awkward when faced with unexpected silences or social hiccups, even when we think there should be nothing awkward about the situation. Calhoun's contrast between practical and epistemic weight gives us a way to understand this: the discomfort we feel as part of awkwardness is an acknowledgment that we care about our attunement to others.

5.9 Conclusion

In the final section of this chapter, I've focused on the parallel responses we might have to awkwardness and shamefulness, allowing ourselves to be affected by them even when we don't endorse the evaluative standpoints from which they issue. In doing so, I've emphasized similarities between awkwardness and shame. But there are important differences, too, and not just in the nature of the experiences themselves. Shame suggests something wrongful about the individual. Recognizing that our reaction is due to awkwardness is important in understanding our normative assessment of the issue at hand, allocating responsibility, and figuring out how to move forward. Experiencing an act as shameful implies a normative judgment, whether or not one endorses it. If I feel ashamed of something, the implication is that I've done something wrong (by some standard, even if not my own).

The same is not true of awkwardness. Shifting our reaction from shame to awkwardness, or understanding that our shame is caused by awkwardness, corrects the impression of personal failure. It allows us to understand the case in terms of having been ill-served by our social resources. One of the many valuable lessons of the social turn in epistemology is the revelation that failures which initially present as individual can in fact turn out to be collective. This discovery lessens the burden on individuals while helping us recognize our potential roles (and limits) in remedying the situation. This might mean creating spaces for discussion, or mapping out paths for conversation. It might mean recognizing and anticipating our awkward feelings as the result of a gap in our collective scripts; expecting and tolerating awkwardness. I'll say more about these possibilities in the next chapter.

But let me close by clarifying: a world where nothing is awkward and everything is discussed is not my goal. In fact, it sounds pretty awful. There are any number of topics I don't want my colleagues, family members, or friends to discuss with me. Awkwardness offers a way of drawing boundaries without the normative judgments implied by shame. But it also represents a way of silencing challenges to problematic norms. The question we're left with, then, is how to move forward given the ambiguity of awkwardness itself: what do we do with it? In the next and final chapter, I offer some suggestions.

6
The Importance of Being Awkward

6.1 Introduction: Where Do We Go from Here?

Throughout the book, I've suggested that awkwardness highlights places where our social scripts are absent or inadequate. This makes it seem like a useful tool. But I've also suggested that awkwardness inhibits the development of social scripts, selectively disadvantages and burdens certain groups, and gets used to shut down conversations and evade accountability. So, where does this leave us with respect to the normative status of awkwardness? And if the remedy for awkwardness is better social scripts, then what exactly is involved in creating them, either collectively or as individuals?

These are big questions, and I can only sketch answers here. But a closer examination of the first (the question of the normative status of awkwardness) offers us a way to make progress on the second (the question of revising our scripts). Many of the problems with awkwardness arise not from its phenomenological qualities, but from our conception of it as attaching to individuals or specific issues rather than the interaction between individuals and social norms. Once we understand the causes of awkwardness, we can deploy it more strategically. We can also find alternative ways of accomplishing the jobs we use it to do. For example, if awkwardness is a way of protecting privacy around certain issues, we can work on claiming our entitlement to that privacy more directly. Or, if awkwardness functions as a way of socially sanctioning people when we can't directly object to their transgressions, as I suggested in chapter 5, we can develop more direct strategies for addressing objectionable behaviors. Awkwardness will never go away completely: it highlights ambiguity in our social roles and scripts; it marks out the areas of social life where we're ambivalent, or uncertain. And even as we resolve these areas, new borders will emerge. This brings us back to the point above: since we can't eliminate awkwardness, we can try to change our relationship to it.

In the first section of the chapter, I describe what that process might involve. I then discuss how we can go about using the insights from awkwardness to improve our social scripts. That's a big question, and the remarks here are intended to be suggestive rather than exhaustive, drawing on work already being done by philosophers working on emotion, conceptual engineering, and social justice. Finally, I talk about areas of everyday life where we're likely to encounter awkwardness: in our work, social, and online lives.

6.2 Awkwardness Revisited

By now I hope to have made a convincing case for the normative significance of awkwardness. I've argued that it can be epistemically useful, drawing our attention to gaps in our social and conceptual resources. But this doesn't mean awkwardness itself is good; I would not call myself an "awkwardness advocate." Nor would I say that awkwardness is intrinsically bad. While it's tempting to think of awkwardness as having an essentially ostracizing function, this is a mistake: yes, awkwardness tends to be attached to individuals, but this is not part of the response itself; like other responses such as disgust, awkwardness lends itself to problematic co-optation.[1] But that may be something we can change.

---

[1] See Kelly 2013 for a discussion of disgust, and for an analysis of the debate between "disgust skeptics" and "disgust advocates."

What would it mean to revisit our attitude toward awkwardness? First, we might change the normative judgments we associate with it, becoming more attentive to the kinds of evaluations it encourages. Because it arises when our social scripts or schemata are disrupted, awkwardness can be pinned on those who don't conform, who challenge our existing norms, or who are observably different, either because of their modes of self-expression or because of features of their physical presentation. At the end of chapter 1, I argued that we should not think of awkwardness as caused by individuals but rather as the result of insufficient social and epistemic resources. Awkward interactions aren't caused by particular people, but by a misfit between people and the social resources available to them.

Here we can return to an idea referenced in chapter 1, the social model of disability. On this view, disability isn't something inherent to a person or their body, it's something that emerges out of a person's interaction with a particular environment.[2] More broadly, the model draws our attention to the ways environments enable or limit our actions, and determine who fits—or misfits. Pohlhaus uses the example of medical schools designed for men—in other words, lacking women's bathrooms:

> While the buildings may have served those who worked there prior to the entry of women students quite well, the entrance of new bodies into the building reveals that it is not suited for enabling all bodies. Moreover, including new bodies into the building does not itself remedy the problem; worse yet, those bodies can appear to produce (rather than simply reveal) a problem. If one does not pay attention to the environment itself as something designed to serve some bodies and not others, the inclusion of new bodies can appear to reveal these new bodies as lacking in

---

[2] For an overview and critique, see Terzi 2004.

themselves, rather than being disabled by an environment that is suited to enable only certain bodies. (2020: 238)[3]

The lesson here is that we should be wary of attributing misfit to individuals, rather than structures or environments. We should also expect that as we include new individuals in our environments, whether built or social, those environments will reveal their insufficiency in ways they haven't yet. And that social environment includes us: writing about interactions with cognitively disabled people, Timpe argues, "What a deaf-blind individual . . . is capable of doing depends on those in her environment, including whether they're able to recognize that potential agency and then work to make possible the opportunity for its expression" (2022: 165).

That work can feel awkward. Becoming more inclusive at work, at school, in our social circles, and in our online discourse may lead to awkwardness; when it does, it's because making progress can reveal the insufficiency of our existing social scripts. Understanding awkwardness as playing this role lets us take advantage of the epistemic opportunity it provides: a chance to test our scripts for areas of exclusion, obscurity, and oppression, and then improve them. I'll say more about what that work involves in sections 6.4 and 6.5, but first I'll highlight two other areas where we should reevaluate awkwardness. The first has to do with how we experience it, and the second has to do with what we do about it.

6.3 Shifting the Blame for Awkwardness

A better understanding of the relationship between social scripts and awkwardness will shift focus from the individual onto the

---

[3] Pohlhaus draws an analogy between the social model of disability and epistemic disablement; in both instances, attention to the environment in which an agent operates (whether physically or epistemically) can help us reconceive constraints on her ability to exercise agency as a matter of disabling infrastructure rather than individual limitations.

situation, and view it not as an individual production but as a collective failure to create better social resources. This shift has implications beyond blame itself: first, changing how we conceptualize the causes of awkwardness has the potential to change how we experience it. Dahl (2018) describes a process of trying to reappraise her experience of cringing as a positive: viewing the embarrassment of "cringeworthy" experiences as a sign of learning and growing. This kind of reappraisal focuses on reinterpreting the physiological markers of emotion, and the cognitions we associate with them—transforming nervous jitters into excitement, to use another of Dahl's examples.

But the reappraisal I have in mind goes beyond this—it's not just transforming what we take ourselves to be experiencing, but what we take it to signify. Munch-Jurisic's (2021: 13593) discussion of anxiety provides a helpful model here:

> our understanding of emotions is mediated through a set of interpretive tools, even when we are not explicitly aware that we are applying them, for example in the case of scripts, biases, heuristics, etc. In sum, the experience of our own bodily feelings and our understanding of other people's affective states (facial expressions, bodily gestures, etc.) is always mediated through our hermeneutic equipment. . . . By implication, this process of understanding, explaining, and predicting our own and others' feelings is an inherently normative endeavor. . . . The internal perspective from which we understand emotions reflects a specific point of view, imbued with a normatively charged set of ideas of how a certain feeling should be construed, categorized, and acted upon.

This "normatively charged" set of ideas is also evident in the way we experience awkwardness: as isolating and an individual failing. My suggestion is that when we reconceptualize awkwardness as something caused from without, rather than within, we may be able to experience it as less aversive, and as directing us to look outside ourselves for the cause. This in turn may make moments of awkwardness feel less alienating.

It might be too much to expect of us to start enjoying awkward moments. It might also be undesirable; our discussion of "awkwardness psychopaths" in chapter 2, and the discussion of how awkwardness can be weaponized in chapter 5, suggest that invulnerability to the discomfort of awkwardness can be dangerous. But even if we can't and shouldn't learn to enjoy awkwardness in the moment it occurs, perhaps we can find its aftermath less torturous, and lessen the cringing sting of awkward memories. If we become better able to tolerate awkwardness over time, we might equip ourselves to construct the kind of social scripts and scaffolding needed to reduce the sorts of situations that give rise to it. If awkwardness becomes less painful to recollect, we might in turn be able to endure it better, and take on the work of confronting it head-on. And for some of us, that work will be an important step in mitigating the social harms discussed throughout the book so far.

This brings us to the second avenue for improvement, which involves what we might think of as, for lack of a better term, the redistribution of social capital. Once we shift our understanding of awkwardness away from the individual and onto the interaction, we open up additional opportunities for remedying the awkwardness, both in the moment and in the future. Long-term strategies might involve addressing our social scripts and their deficiencies. Short-term work will involve getting the interaction back on track. Given that awkwardness emerges from new forms of social interaction and confronting existing but unaddressed social issues, we should consider who incurs the burden of that awkwardness. This might seem in tension with what I've just said—isn't the whole point to shift the focus away from individuals? But recall the point in section 3.2 that executing unfamiliar social maneuvers often feels awkward and looks clumsy. The question then becomes, when we have to do things awkwardly—when awkwardness is inevitable—who bears the cost?

6.4 Scripts, Culture, and Conceptual Engineering

Our reliance on scripts, and the claim that we "make," "create," or "revise" them, has been a recurring theme throughout the book. In chapter 3, I said a bit about how we do this, and in chapter 4, I argued that we lack adequate scripts for navigating issues around moral critique. In this final chapter, I want to come back to this idea and look at some more specific examples.

First, consider a case of effortfully adopting a new script. In recent years, spurred by concerns about bias in the hiring process, many academic hiring committees have changed their first-round interviewing process to eliminate small talk and follow-up questions. In these departments, all candidates are now asked the same questions in the same order. From the interviewer's perspective, this feels awkward.[4] We might bemoan the artificiality of the interaction, the loss of conversational back-and-forth; we might feel our performance is stilted and we're unable to be as friendly or natural as we otherwise would be. But job interviews are going to make someone (or everyone) feel awkward. If making things less awkward for the candidate means making it more awkward for the committee, that's as it should be. While the days of hotel-room interviews and mingling at the APA Smoker might not have felt awkward for more senior members of the profession, they

---

[4] I can't speak to this new interview experience from a candidate's perspective, having been a candidate back in the era of hotel-room interviews at the Eastern APA. This model was, unsurprisingly, quite awkward for many of us candidates. However, in discussing awkwardness with colleagues, a number have brought up scripted interviews, unprompted, as an example of an experience that feels awkward, so I hope the reader will allow me this piece of anecdata.

most certainly felt awkward, or worse, to many others. In cases like these, making things better and fairer means choosing your awkward: who will feel awkward, and where, and when? Faced with that question, I suggest the answer should be: those with the most power and social capital; those whose social standing and reputation can withstand it. If feeling awkward is the cost of social change, it should be borne by those with social advantage—in this case, those in positions of professional power.

The interview example shows how the creation and negotiation of scripts can be explicit. In recent years, the philosophical literature on conceptual engineering has taken off, though the practice itself predates the invention of the term (see Chalmers 2020 for a brief history). While the idea of explicitly and effortfully revising concepts isn't quite the same as revising a script, doing one expands the set of resources we can draw on in doing the other. For example, re-engineering the concept of "illness" so that it includes "mental illness" expands our set of scripts for asking for time off of work, or requesting accommodations at school. At a broad level, we can change the meaning we attach to certain cultural or social practices; this affects their significance, but also the way they interact with social roles and norms. For example, Bicchieri describes a Sudanese campaign to change attitudes toward female genital cutting by introducing new terminology, "reframing the conversation about girls' bodies" by describing them as "whole, intact, healthy" rather in terms of chasteness or lack thereof (2017: 139–140).

When we engineer a concept, we gain access to a whole new set of resources associated with that expanded meaning (recall the discussion in section 5.2 of coopting existing terms like "depression" to explain women's postpartum symptoms). Nor is the role of a concept so different from the role of a script: as Brigandt and Rosario (2020: 101) write, "By 'concepts' in general we mean components of a person's thought which can influence reasoning as well as action. Concepts have the latter capacity by means of embodying descriptive and/or normative beliefs (some of which may be implicit)."

This job description aptly characterizes the work done by scripts, at least in the sense I've been using the term throughout this book. And just as conceptual engineering asks questions about the ways in which concepts can be useful or defective, attending to awkwardness opens up corresponding questions about which scripts serve our purposes, achieve or hinder our normative goals, and so on.[5]

The literature on conceptual engineering is one place to look for lessons as to how we might improve social scripts for things like moral criticism. Our discussion (in chapter 4) of Zheng's distinction between formative and summative criticism offers an example of what such engineering might look like. (And note that, like the example of postpartum depression referenced above, Zheng's distinction adapts conceptual material used in a different context: in this case, educational assessment.) By refining our concept of criticism to distinguish the aim of assessment from the aim of improvement, we can find a way to communicate agents' moral shortcomings without "the sting of blame" (Zheng 2021: 517). This is not likely to be accomplished with in-the-moment improvisation. But once the concept is "in circulation," so to speak, it's accessible enough that we can invoke it to reduce the potential awkwardness of misunderstood attempts at criticism. We don't have to do so by name—I'm not suggesting that "formative moral criticism" is going to gain widespread traction. But the idea that there's a version of moral critique that doesn't involve taking its object to be blameworthy, and that aims at improvement, allows us to attach a different meaning to a familiar activity and allows our criticism to be received differently.

Changing scripts requires recognizing where and how they operate. In some cases, we can anticipate potential conflicts or awkwardness and plan for it. In the case of changing how we conduct job interviews, for example, we know that adopting the new script

---

[5] For an overview of conceptual engineering and conceptual ethics, see the papers collected in Burgess, Capellen, and Plunkett 2020, especially the editors' introduction.

will be awkward; by explaining our reasons for conducting the interview this way, we contextualize the awkwardness as a necessary step in creating a fairer process.

In cases like these, the process of shifting scripts is gradual and intentional. It can also be effortful, requiring changes to our existing habits and routines. Consciously following a script may, in these cases, seem to make things *more* awkward, because we've internalized certain existing scripts so well. But this is a consequence of the fact that our extant scripts didn't serve everyone, and that sometimes awkwardness is an inevitable stage in transitioning to more inclusive or fairer scripts. For example, many of us now take time at the beginning of a new class, or a meeting, to share our pronouns and invite students to share theirs. A professor might introduce the script by modeling it: "my name is Professor Plakias, and I use "she/her" pronouns." This may initially feel awkward for some of us whose pronouns match our presentation in the workplace. But for people who regularly have to choose between being misgendered and correcting others, it's been awkward for a while.

The pronoun example also shows how technology can mediate, and in some cases ameliorate, awkwardness: many professors and students include pronouns in their email signatures, and when meetings and classes shifted to Zoom, people took the opportunity to add pronouns to their screen names, reducing the need to explicitly state them and/or correct others' mistakes.

This brings us back to the question that led into this section: who bears the costs of awkwardness? The example of building pronouns into introductions reminds us that what often seems like extra work—the work of adopting scripts—is actually a shift in who's doing the labor. Our practice of *not* inquiring into pronouns, or of having gender-binary rather than gender-neutral bathrooms, puts quite a lot of work onto certain individuals and groups: the work of correcting people's pronoun usage (or opting not to correct, and tolerating being misgendered); the work of performing risk assessments every time one needs to use a bathroom. Explicitly asking and stating pronouns might seem awkward because it disrupts a routine that has become automatic—it involves adopting a script that is new to us. But the work involved—the effort of stopping to notice pronouns—is not new. It's just been done in ways that were, up until recently, invisible to those now performing it.

I've used the example of pronouns and of job interviews because they're cases where the script metaphor translates quite literally: we go to trainings that suggest actual verbal scripts we can use in work or classroom settings. It's worth noting that not everyone agrees on which script to use, or whether to explicitly ask for pronouns at all. When an issue is both morally fraught and ambiguous—when we desire to respect others' gender identities but we don't know how best to do it—things get awkward.

6.5 Awkwardness and the Art of Social Improv

So far, the approaches we've discussed are explicit and effortful. But what about more spontaneous strategies? Humor is one tactic, though it's a short-term fix rather than a long-term solution. By "humor," I don't (just) mean cringe comedy, like the kind we discussed in chapter 3. Nor do I mean nervous laughter, which is not an expression of genuine mirth (see Olin 2022). Humor is an effective way of negotiating potentially awkward interpersonal interactions because it evokes intimacy. It's not just that laughter relieves tension (though it does)—it reinforces the idea of a shared set of social bonds and knowledge. To be able to laugh at oneself, or at some shared object of mirth, reinforces our security and sense of social belonging, a sense that could otherwise be destabilized or threatened by awkward interactions (Dunbar 2022). As I pointed out in chapter 3, it also coordinates our emotional experiences, if only for a moment: when we're both genuinely laughing, we're both having the same feeling, expressing it in a way we mutually recognize; in virtue of that experience, the uncertainty of awkwardness is broken. It's also very hard to remain self-conscious while laughing. So, humor or jokes can be a way of smoothing over the potentially alienating effects of awkwardness when we're unable to find the script we need, and we have no choice but to just face the awkwardness.

Another option in these cases is to acknowledge or "own" the fact that a situation is awkward. "Owning" something is admittedly not a concept common to philosophical discourse, but Whitcomb et al. (2017: 517) offer a useful characterization in their analysis of intellectual humility. According to their account, to "own" one's intellectual limitations involves "dispositions to: (1) believe that one has them; and to believe that their negative outcomes are due to them; (2) to admit or acknowledge them; (3) to care about them and take them seriously; and (4) to feel regret or dismay, but not hostility, about them." Their analysis is aimed at a trait or characteristic—they argue that we should own our epistemic limitations—but we can modify it for our purposes: owning an awkward situation involves believing or recognizing that the situation or interaction is or was awkward; acknowledging or admitting that fact; caring about it and taking it seriously; and feeling regret, dismay, or at least a desire to do better next time. It doesn't require claiming that we are awkward, though it does involve recognizing our own responsibility for making things awkward.

Why does this help? Well, as we've noted at various points, one way to defuse awkwardness is to acknowledge it. Once we do that, we shift the script from "undefined" to something else—embarrassment, perhaps. Given that this seems like a relatively easy way to defuse awkward situations, why don't we do it more often? One explanation is that owning awkwardness is socially costly: it involves taking a hit to one's veneer of social smoothness. Just as admitting ignorance incurs a cost to one's epistemic reputation, admitting awkwardness incurs a cost to one's social reputation. As we saw in chapter 3, this can have the paradoxical effect of elevating one's social status, since only a really confident person would admit to being so awkward. But that's a risky move, and takes a certain amount of social standing to pull off. Rather than thinking of owning awkwardness as something we do as individuals, we might think of it as a way of collectively redistributing social capital. Awkward moments are an opportunity for social inclusion, a way to acknowledge the difficulty surrounding certain topics and share the burden of navigating them. Owning awkwardness is one way to do this.

Getting out of an awkward interaction requires getting onto a script. Coordinating or even creating scripts on the spot involves a kind of improvisation: we perform an action or an utterance that invites our social partner(s) to join us in adopting a script, thereby transforming an awkward situation into a more familiar one. Resolving awkwardness can involve a bid to relate in terms of an existing script—the "small talk about the weather" script; the "eye contact and smile" script, if I'm passing someone on the street. This is why identifying common interests is a useful strategy for ameliorating awkwardness (Clegg 2012a, 2012b): it puts us in familiar territory. The resolution can also involve choosing a role—or helping someone else find theirs. The hardware store owner who tries commiserating with my husband ("oh boy, what's she got you working on now?") is attempting to smooth out a potentially awkward interaction, and the fact that we take him up on it shows that the desire for social smoothness sometimes outweighs our deeper normative commitments. (I abhor being cast as the nagging wife, yet I play along anyway.)

How do we do this? It sounds simple (it's not simple), but we start, and hope others follow. Changing or introducing a script in a given situation—mid-scene, as it were—is like making a move in improv: you put it out there, and count on your partner to be cooperative. In her book *Cringeworthy*, the science writer Melissa Dahl describes confronting her fear of embarrassment; one of the pivotal moments involves an improv comedy class. Dahl points out that the "yes and..." rule of improv allows us to commit both to the performance itself and to each other. This coordination allows us to pick up a social script mid-interaction, and it helps explain why awkward moments don't stay awkward forever. The previous chapters have argued that social interaction is a type of performance. And the dynamics of conversational exchanges as involving a series of bids made by speakers is itself familiar philosophical ground, from which I'll borrow to illustrate how we make our way out of awkward situations.

Conversations, for example, can be understood as a series of moves involving a "common ground" of information (Stalnaker 1978). In any given exchange, there's a set of shared beliefs on which the conversation can rely. Speakers' utterances function, in part, as bids to add new information to the common ground, or as ways of testing what's in the common ground, and so on. My suggestion is that this offers us a model on which to understand how scripts coordinate: they provide a common ground for our social interactions, but instead of (just) containing propositions, they contain norms, roles, and event sequences; certain acts, utterances, gestures, or even facial expressions shift the script, in the same way that an utterance might shift the common ground of a conversation. This allows us to improvise scripts for certain topics.

Following Stalnaker, let's call one of these improvisatory moves a *bid*.[6] When we make a bid, we're proposing a script and inviting others to join us in enacting it. This script can be a new one—one we're creating on the spot—or it can involve amending an existing script. Or it might be a familiar script that we default to.

The reference to improv comedy above might give the wrong impression: improvisation isn't always effortful, or "big." We improvise a lot. It's "arguably our default way of being in the world," since

---

[6] After writing this section, I noticed that Riggle (2017) uses the same terminology in his account of awesomeness as creating social openings, but the sense in which we use it is slightly different. I think the spirit of our usage is similar, in that we're both interested in how social interactions can be adjusted or improvised on the fly.

even mundane and familiar activities like handwriting involve making slight adjustments to our gestures and performances—"micro-improvisations" like changing the pace of our walk to avoid (or catch up with) a neighbor (Kreuger & Salice 2021: 51). Importantly, improvisation occurs even within scripted activities; because our scripts don't cover the various contingencies that arise in social situations, we're often unaware of the lacunae in our plans until one catches us off-guard. Our scripts constrain a class of actions available to us, but given the contingencies against which these unfold, we require a degree of plasticity in how we implement them, and this is where improvisation comes into play. And just like in improv comedy, when it comes to social interaction, a successful bid requires the complicity—however implicit and unspoken—of others.

A basic and familiar bid involves the way we frequently shift situations from awkward to embarrassing by proclaiming it to be so: "well, this is embarrassing!" This resolves any ambiguity about whether we're aware of the problem; in doing so, we offer others a script for responding—they then reassure us, maybe say something like "that happens to me all the time, don't worry!" or "we've all been there!" In fact, we can do the same thing by labeling a situation awkward. Saying "this is awkward!" is itself a bid to shift to an embarrassment script, calling for reassurance or laughter, bringing us back on track. Awkwardness is ironic like this: once it's named, it can disappear. (Not always—I was sure telling people "I'm writing a book on awkwardness" would be a great icebreaker at awkward social gatherings; in fact, it only works about half the time, and when it fails, things get *really* awkward.) Naming awkwardness has the power to transform it into embarrassment, by signaling to others that we're aware of the situation and our failure to successfully navigate it. If our bid is accepted, we can then move forward together, following the script for embarrassment and laughing it off. This doesn't have to involve embarrassment; other emotion scripts, such as anger, frustration, or mirth, can work as well. What matters is that when we name and mutually acknowledge awkwardness, we're coordinating on something, which is one way to shift out of the awkward moment into more familiar social territory. (Which is not to say the awkwardness will be forgotten—as we noted in chapter 2, the memory of awkwardness can persist for years.) If our bid fails, things remain awkward, and probably get even more awkward.

Making a bid requires confidence—and skill. When we make a bid to shift a script, we take charge of the awkward situation; we're offering each other a way out. But doing so makes us vulnerable. It opens us up to social rejection. If we're trying something really new, we can no longer rely on our "assigned social role" or existing script. Riggle (2016) argues that the social virtue we call awesomeness consists in something like this: "the art of creating social openings," which allow us to step outside the generic roles assigned to us by extant social scripts. This is awesome, Riggle says, because it allows us to express our individuality and creates opportunities for others to do the same. That's not quite what I'm describing here, because a bid is just as likely (if not more so) to rely on a repurposed script or role; we shouldn't expect an element of innovation or individuality. In fact, resolving awkwardness might make things significantly *less* awesome by putting someone in an outdated role or co-opting an undesirable script—the nagging wife and long-suffering husband, to return to our earlier example. But even if we're not being awesome, offering someone else a social opening acknowledges their need for one—and that in itself is an act of social recognition.

The term "awesome" suggests there's something supererogatory about creating these openings. But by failing to rescue someone from awkwardness when we otherwise might (here I'm thinking of situations where we could do so at relatively little cost to ourselves), we leave them out in the social cold. And while a single instance might not seem like much, these instances of social isolation accrue; over time, failing to remedy awkwardness can amount to social harm (Brownlee 2020a, 2020b). The question of who steps in and makes a bid, or incurs the awkwardness of effortfully executing an unfamiliar script, is at least partly the question of how to distribute this risk of social harm.

There are other specific strategies we might adopt in addition to these. First, we can coin or co-opt a term or concept. Having a shorthand for something is a way to circumvent, or at least condense, awkward conversation and the job of describing it. Here, the "script" we need is really a concept or term: having the term "microaggression," for example, might help a female graduate student convey how a classmate's comments made her feel without requiring her to elaborate the whole experience, navigate questions about what was and wasn't explicitly stated, explain how the comments affected her, and so on.

The writer Kyleigh Leddy describes her struggle with finding the words to talk about the death of her sister: "I wished there was a word to identify myself in relation to my loss. I longed for a label that would be instantly understood by others, one that would communicate both Kait's presence and absence in my life. I wanted a word like *orphan* or *widow*—a term that says, 'I once had a sibling, but I lost her.'" Leddy goes on to describe how isolating it is to lack such a word; how having one would allow her to connect with others experiencing similar losses. But the word she seeks will also empower her to control when and what she shares: "At the very least, I wanted a term that could serve as a metaphorical stop sign in conversation: a warning to tread carefully, a succinct and sufficient answer in its own right" (Leddy 2023).

Online communities can be helpful here. By extending access to conversations, support, and conceptual resources, they provide space for having difficult conversations, and allow us to hone our interactions in ways that might come in handy in future face-to-face spaces.

6.6 Awkwardness Online

Like the consciousness-raising groups discussed in chapter 5, online communities build in the assumption of dealing with difficult issues, and offer the opportunity to explicitly coin terminology and outline rules for interaction under conditions where discomfort is an expected part of the process. These are especially useful in contexts where the social norms around an issue are unclear or discourage open conversation. For example, disclosing a pregnancy in the first trimester is often discouraged or, in some cultures, outright tabooed. As a result, women who experience first-trimester miscarriage often lack social support and are left to navigate the experience on their own (see Aquien 2021). Discussing the role played by online discussion boards, Hardy and Kukla note, "women who have had a miscarriage may feel that their reactions and experiences do not make sense or fit into a rational and recognizable story that can be publicly consumed or produced. The boards can be used as a place both to express this frustration and to try to forge this kind of articulable sense. In turn, others give uptake that affirms women's reactions as meaningful, appropriate, and comprehensible" (2015: 111).

Online communities help people develop and share emotion scripts that shape their own understanding, as well as scripts to deploy in potentially awkward offline interactions. But an interaction's taking place online is no immunization against feeling awkward; we can still end up wondering whether an interaction was successful, whether a joke landed, or why no one has reacted to our latest post. Online interactions also lack access to some of the physical cues we use to coordinate scripts. In chapter 1, I talked about the way that gaze, proxemics, and conversational timing act as social cues. They also offer hints about how well a conversational exchange is going—whether a joke is well-received; whether someone is sympathetic to our complaints. Online, we can't rely on these cues, but we can't be thrown off by them, either.

But just as being online doesn't immunize us against awkwardness, it doesn't guarantee that what we end up with will represent progress. Ashton (2021) points out that while online discourse is a good way of gathering diverse epistemic perspectives, it's lacking when it comes to opportunities for "collaborative critical reflection." In other words, we can easily find out what other people think about, say, reclining seat backs on airplanes, or the ethics of cultural appropriation. But doing so doesn't guarantee epistemic progress or even insight. In the next and final section, I discuss why sometimes eliminating awkwardness might be the wrong goal.

6.7 After Awkward?

Effortfully adopting a new script, as in the case of pronouns, or job interviews, is a helpful reminder that awkwardness is the result of shifting our routines and habits, and changing how we interact with our social environment. This environment includes other people, but while they're witnesses to the awkwardness, and hence implicated in it in a way—things wouldn't be awkward if we were alone—they're not the cause of it. So, there's a double benefit to engineering and adopting new scripts: they simultaneously improve our stock of social resources by giving us tools to avoid future awkwardness, and they can remind us of the causes of awkwardness, helping to shift how we think about and experience it.

We sometimes actively debate social scripts and how we ought to revise them. These debates increasingly play out online: it seems like every few weeks, the Internet will become preoccupied with a question of etiquette, like whether it's okay to recline your seat on a plane. In these cases, consensus is rare, so we rarely settle the debate—instead, we make people feel more confident in the correctness of their opinion. But this isn't always a good thing. Sometimes, awkwardness is preferable to the alternatives. Consider the airplane case: is it permissible to ask someone to put their seat up a bit? Having "pre-negotiated" the question (by debating it on the Internet) doesn't guarantee that we're on the same page when the issue arises, but it will make us more confident that we are following, if not *the* script, *a* script. In other words, it will make us feel less awkward, knowing as we do that our behavior is in line with some socially accepted norm. But the relevant question when it comes time to act is not, is there some norm, somewhere, according to which my behavior is acceptable? It's: what's the norm here? Knowing that someone on the Internet endorses the norm of reclining a seat, or shushing someone else's child in a restaurant, may boost my confidence that my actions are justifiable—but it doesn't guarantee or even make it more likely that my neighbor agrees. This combination of confidence and disagreement makes for something more combustible than awkwardness: anger, resentment, contempt. Faced with those alternatives, awkwardness may look more palatable. This recalls a point made in chapter 4: awkwardness can prevent premature certainty, keeping us from landing on a moral judgment or social script before we're in an epistemic position to do so.

The lesson here is that eliminating awkwardness is not, in itself, the goal. Instead, we should focus on noticing where it arises—which subjects are awkward to discuss? Who do we find it awkward to interact with, and when?—and taking opportunities to develop better scripts for those areas of our lives.

6.8 Conclusion

Reading the previous chapters, one could conclude that eliminating awkwardness is an improvement: we'll expand our repertoire of social scripts, make it easier for people to communicate and coordinate, and the result will be progress. Of course, this is too simple. What awkwardness transforms into might be something much less pleasant. For example, the hesitancy of awkwardness might give way to the confidence of anger. Awkwardness acts as a backstop against certainty and entitlement. It prevents intrusion into certain areas of people's lives, by keeping us unsure of whether we have standing to criticize or confront them.

That's not to say awkwardness is good. It's just, sometimes, less bad. In settings like an airplane, or a public restroom, awkwardness is preferable to anger or shame. Recall Goffman's observation that embarrassment is a sacrifice of individual composure on behalf of society: the embarrassed person loses face; social order gains flexibility. Here, we might think of awkwardness as a sacrifice we make to keep the idea of public versus private space intact. When nothing is awkward, nothing is private; nothing is public, either.

The question is not, is awkwardness good? It's, what is awkwardness good for? In light of the remarks I've just made, one might expect the answer to involve privacy: awkwardness is a way of drawing a boundary around the areas of our experience we don't wish to share. And it does function that way, sometimes. But because awkwardness signals ambiguity, it would be better to explicitly claim our privacy, or explicitly state that the topic should be publicly discussed. Awkwardness is the "um" of feelings: it buys us time to figure out what we really want to say, and to work up the resolve to say it.[7] In other words, awkwardness is not a stable strategy for delineating the private from the public. It's a transitional, temporary fix when we're trying to figure out where the line should be drawn—or when we know where it should be drawn but lack the social, hermeneutical, or other resources needed to actually draw it.

Insofar as awkwardness helps mark off boundaries, and lets people know when they've crossed them, a world without awkwardness might not be one we'd want to live in. But that's not to let it off the hook. It's a transitional, unstable state, pointing us to a problem that needs solving. And it'll be with us as long as we are dependent on norms to guide us, and as long as those norms change and evolve. Awkwardness isn't going anywhere.

---

[7] See Enfield 2017 for a discussion of the different functions of "um" versus "uh" in this respect.

Bibliography

Abelson, R. 1981. The Psychological Status of the Script Concept. *American Psychologist* 36(7): 715–729.
Ahmed, S. 2014. Not in the Mood. *New Formations: A Journal of Culture/Theory/Politics* 82: 13–28.
Ahmed, S. 2019. A Complaint Biography. *Biography* 42(3): 514–523. https://doi.org/. doi:10.1353/bio.2019.0057.
Alcoff, L. 2007. Epistemologies of Ignorance: Three Types. In *Race and Epistemologies of Ignorance*, edited by Shannon Sullivan & Nancy Tuana, 39–57. State University of New York Press.
Anderson, E. 1995. Feminist Epistemology: An Interpretation and a Defense. *Hypatia* 10(3): 50–84.
Anderson, E. 2000. Beyond Homo Economicus: New Developments in Theories of Social Norms. *Philosophy and Public Affairs* 29(2): 170–200.
Anderson, E. 2016. The Social Epistemology of Morality: Learning from the Forgotten History of the Abolition of Slavery. In *The Epistemic Life of Groups*, edited by M. Fricker & M. Brady, 75–94. Oxford University Press.
Anderson, L. 2017. Hermeneutical Impasses. *Philosophical Topics* 45(2): 1–20.
Aquien, J. 2021. *Trois mois sur silence* [in French]. Payot.
Argyle, M. 1990. *Bodily Communication*. Routledge (first published 1975, Methuen & Co).
Argyle, M., Lefebvre, L., & Cook, M. 1974. The Meaning of Five Patterns of Gaze. *European Journal of Social Psychology* 4: 125–136. https://doi.org/10.1002/ejsp.2420040202.
Aronson, E., Willerman, B., & Floyd, J. 1966. The Effect of a Pratfall on Increasing Interpersonal Attractiveness. *Psychonomic Science* 4(6): 227–228.
Arpaly, N. 2003. *Unprincipled Virtue*. Oxford University Press.
Ashton, N. 2021. Coronavirus, Online Communities, and Social Change. *Public Ethics Blog*, February 8, 2021. https://www.publicethics.org/post/coronavirus-online-communities-and-social-change. Accessed 3/15/22.
Bailey, A. 2018. On Anger, Silence and Epistemic Injustice. *Royal Institute of Philosophy Supplement* 84: 93–115.
Baker, M., Hamlberstam, Y. Kroft, K., Mas, A., & Messacar, D. Pay Transparency and the Gender Gap. *American Economic Journal: Applied Economics* 15(2): 157–183.

Baumeister, R., & Leary, M. 1995. The Need to Belong: Desire for Interpersonal Attachments as a Fundamental Human Motivation. *Psychological Bulletin* 117(3): 497–529.

Beattie, G. W., Cutler, A., & Pearson, M. 1982. Why Is Mrs. Thatcher Interrupted So Often? *Nature* 300(5894): 744–747.

Beebee, H. 2013. Women and Deviance in Philosophy. In *Women in Philosophy: What Needs to Change?*, edited by K. Hutchison & F. Jenkins, 61–80. Oxford: Oxford University Press.

Beer, J. S., Heerey, E. A., Keltner, D., Scabini, D., & Knight, R. T. 2003. The Regulatory Function of Self-Conscious Emotion: Insights from Patients with Orbitofrontal Damage. *Journal of Personality and Social Psychology* 85(4): 594–604.

Benziman, Y. 2020. Embarrassment. *Journal of Value Inquiry* 54(1): 77–89.

Berenstain, N. 2020. White Feminist Gaslighting. *Hypatia* 35(4): 733–758.

Berlant, L. 2017. Humorlessness: Three Monologues and a Hairpiece. *Critical Inquiry* 43(2): 305–340.

Berlant, L., & Ngai, S. 2017. Comedy Has Issues. *Critical Inquiry* 43(2): 233–249.

Berthoz, S., Armony, J. L., Blair, R. J. R., and Dolan, R. J. 2002. An fMRI Study of Intentional and Unintentional (Embarrassing) Violations of Social Norms. *Brain* 125(8): 1696–1708.

Bicchieri, C. 2006. *The Grammar of Society*. Cambridge University Press.

Bicchieri, C. 2008. The Fragility of Fairness: An Experimental Investigation on the Conditional Status of Pro-Social Norms. *Philosophical Issues* 18(1): 229–248.

Bicchieri, C. 2016. *Norms in the Wild*. Oxford University Press.

Bicchieri, C., & McNally, P. 2018. Shrieking Sirens: Schemata, Scripts, and Social Norms; How Change Occurs. *Social Philosophy and Policy* 35(1): 23–53.

Billig, M. 2001. Humor and Embarrassment: Limits of "Nice Guy" Theories of Social Life. *Theory, Culture and Society* 18(5): 23–43.

Blair, R. J. R, Sellars, C., Strickland, I., Clark, F., Williams, A. O., Smith, M., & Jones, L. 1995. Emotion Attributions in the Psychopath. *Personality and Individual Differences* 19(4): 431–437.

Brennan, G., Eriksson, L., Goodin, R., & Southwood, N. 2013. *Explaining Norms*. Oxford University Press.

Brandt, A., & Rozin, P. 1997. *Morality and Health*. Routledge.

Brigandt, I., & Rosario, E. 2020. Strategic Conceptual Engineering for Epistemic and Social Aims. In *Conceptual Engineering and Conceptual Ethics*, edited by A. Burgess, H. Cappelen, & D. Plunkett, 100–124. Oxford University Press.

Brownlee, K. 2020a. *Being Sure of Each Other: An Essay on Social Rights and Freedoms*. Oxford University Press.

Brownlee, K. 2020b. Social Needs Are a Human Right. OUP Blog, July 10, 2020. https://blog.oup.com/2020/07/social-needs-are-a-human-right/. Accessed 2/17/22.

Burgess, A., Capellen, H., & Plunkett, D., eds. 2020. *Conceptual Engineering and Conceptual Ethics*. Oxford University Press.

Buss, A. H., & Briggs, S. R. 1984. Drama and the Self in Social Interaction. *Journal of Personality and Social Psychology* 47(6): 1310–1324.

Cacioppo, J., & Patrick, W. 2008. *Loneliness: Human Nature and the Need for Social Connection*. Norton.

Calhoun, C. 2004. An Apology for Moral Shame. *Journal of Political Philosophy* 12(2): 127–146.

Calhoun, C. 2016. *Moral Aims*. Oxford University Press.

Campbell, S. 1994. Being Dismissed: The Politics of Emotional Expression. *Hypatia* 9(3): 46–65.

Carroll, N. Horror and Humor. 1999. *Journal of Aesthetics and Art Criticism* 57(2): 145–160.

Catala, A., Fouchet, L., & Poirier, P. 2021. Autism, Epistemic Injustice, and Epistemic Disablement: A Relational Account of Epistemic Agency. *Synthese* 199(3–4): 9013–9039.

Chalmers, D. 2020. What Is Conceptual Engineering and What Should It Be? *Inquiry*. https://doi.org/10.1080/0020174X.2020.1817141.

Chapman, H. A., & Anderson, A. K. 2013. Things Rank and Gross in Nature: A Review and Synthesis of Moral Disgust. *Psychological Bulletin* 139(2): 300.

Cheek, J. M., & Briggs, S. R. 1990. Shyness as a Personality Trait. In *Shyness and Embarrassment: Perspectives from Social Psychology*, edited by R. Crozier, 338–356. Cambridge University Press.

Cheek, J. M., & Buss, A. H. 1981. Shyness and Sociability. *Journal of Personality and Social Psychology* 41(2): 330–339.

Cialdini, R. B., Reno, R. R., & Kallgren, C. A. 1990. A Focus Theory of Normative Conduct: Recycling the Concept of Norms to Reduce Littering in Public Places. *Journal of Personality and Social Psychology* 58(6): 1015–1026.

Clegg, J. 2012a. Stranger Situations: Examining a Self-Regulatory Model of Socially Awkward Encounters. *Group Processes and Intergroup Relations* 15(6): 693–712. https://doi.org/10.1177/1368430212441637.

Clegg, J. 2012b. The Importance of Feeling Awkward: A Dialogical Narrative Phenomenology of Socially Awkward Situations. *Qualitative Research in Psychology* 9(3): 262–278. https://doi.org/10.1080/14780887.2010.500357.

Crerar, C. 2016. Taboo, Hermeneutical Injustice, and Expressively Free Environments. *Episteme* 13(2): 195–207.

Crozier, R. 1990. Introduction. In *Shyness and Embarrassment: Perspectives from Social Psychology*, edited by R. Crozier, 1–15. Cambridge University Press.

Dahl, M. 2018. *Cringeworthy*. Portfolio/Penguin.
Dalton, A. N., Chartrand, T. L., & Finkel, E. J. 2010. The Schema-Driven Chameleon: How Mimicry Affects Executive and Self-Regulatory Resources. *Journal of Personality and Social Psychology* 98(4): 605–617.
Danovich, T. Pre-Peeled Oranges: What Some Call "Lazy," Others Call "A Lifesaver." *NPR: The Salt*, March 7. https://www.npr.org/sections/thesalt/2016/03/07/469521879/pre-peeled-oranges-what-some-call-lazy-others-call-a-lifesaver
Darley, J., & Latané, B. 1968. Bystander Intervention and the Diffusion of Responsibility. *Journal of Personality and Social Psychology* 8(4): 377–383.
D'Arms, J., & Jacobson, D. 2000. The Moralistic Fallacy: On the "Appropriateness" of Emotions. *Philosophy and Phenomenological Research* 61(1): 65–90.
Daston, L. 2022. *Rules: A Short History*. Princeton University Press.
de Groot, P., Frissen, M., de Clercq, N., & Nieudorp, M. 2017. Fecal Microbiota Transplantation in Metabolic Syndrome: History, Present, and Future. *Gut Microbes* 8(3): 253–267.
Deigh, J. 1983. Shame and Self-Esteem: A Critique. *Ethics* 93(2): 225–245.
Doggett, T. 2022. Letting Others Do Wrong. *Nous* 56(1): 40–56.
Doris, J. 2002. *Lack of Character*. Oxford University Press.
Dotson, K. 2011. Tracking Epistemic Violence, Tracking Practices of Silencing. *Hypatia* 26: 236–257. https://doi.org/10.1111/j.1527-2001.2011.01177.x.
Driver, J. 2015. Individual Consumption and Moral Complicity. In *The Moral Complexities of Eating Meat*, edited by B. Bramble & B. Fischer, 67–79. Oxford University Press.
Dunbar, R. 2004. Gossip in Evolutionary Perspective. *Review of General Psychology* 8(2): 100–110.
Dunbar, R. I. M. 2022. Laughter and Its Role in the Evolution of Human Social Bonding. *Philosophical Transactions of the Royal Society B* 377(1863): 20210176.
Eickers, G. 2023. Coordinating Behaviors: Is Social Interaction Scripted? *Journal of the Theory of Social Behavior* 53(1): 83–99.
Eickers, G., & Prinz, J. 2020. Emotion Recognition as a Social Skill. In *The Routledge Handbook of Philosophy of Skill and Expertise*, edited by E. Fridland & C. Pavese, 347–361. Routledge.
Elster, J. 1989. Social Norms and Economic Theory. *Journal of Economic Perspectives* 3(4): 99–117.
Elster, J. 1994. Rationality, Emotions, and Social Norms. *Synthese* 98(1): 21–49.
Enfield, N. J. 2017. *How We Talk: Making Sense of Negotiation*. Basic Books.
Fehr, B. & Russell, J. 1984. Concept of Emotion Viewed From a Prototype Perspective. *Journal of Experimental Psychology* 113(3): 464–486.
Fessler, D. 2007. From Appeasement to Conformity: Evolutionary and Cultural Perspectives on Shame, Competition, and Cooperation. In *The*

Self-Conscious Emotions: Theory and Research, edited by R. Robins, J. Tracy, & J. P.Tangney, 174–193. Guilford Press.

Fileva, I. 2020. You Disgust Me. Or Do You? On the Very Idea of Moral Disgust. *Australasian Journal of Philosophy* 99(1): 19–33. https://doi.org/10.1080/00048402.2020.1717560.

Fischer, J., & Fredricks, R. 2020. The Creeps as a Moral Emotion. *Ergo: An Open Access Journal of Philosophy* 7(6): 191–217.

Fischer, R. 2016. Disgust as Heuristic. *Ethical Theory and Moral Practice* 19(3):679–693.

Fischer, R. 2014. Disgust and the Collection of Bovine Fetal Blood. In *Animal Ethics and Philosophy: Questioning the Orthodoxy*, edited by E. Aaltola & J. Hadley, 151–164. Rowman & Littlefield International.

Fricker, M. 2007. *Epistemic Injustice*. Oxford University Press.

Friedman, M. 1989. Friendship and Moral Growth. *Journal of Value Inquiry* 23(1): 3–14.

Frye, M. 1983. A Note on Anger. In *The Politics of Reality: Essays in Feminist Theory*. The Crossing Press.

Garber, M. 2017. The Weaponization of Awkwardness. *The Atlantic*, December 15. https://www.theatlantic.com/entertainment/archive/2017/12/the-weaponization-of-awkwardness/548291/

Gaut, B. 1993. The Paradox of Horror. *British Journal of Aesthetics* 33(4).

Gilbert, M. 1990. Walking Together: A Paradigmatic Social Phenomenon. *Midwest Studies in Philosophy* 15(1): 1–14.

Goffman, E. 1956. Embarrassment and Social Organization. *American Journal of Sociology* 62(3): 264–271.

Goffman, E. 1959. *The Presentation of the Self in Everyday Life*. Anchor.

Goffman, E. 1963. *Stigma: Notes on the Management of Spoiled Identity*. Simon & Schuster.

Goldberg, S. 2020. *Conversational Pressure*. Oxford University Press.

Grossman, R. B. 2015. Judgments of Social Awkwardness from Brief Exposure to Children with and without High-Functioning Autism. *Autism* 19: 580–587.

Hall, E. 1968. Proxemics. *Current Anthropology* 9(2–3): 83–95.

Harbin, A. 2016. *Disorientation and Moral Life*. Oxford University Press.

Hardy, S., & Kukla, Q. 2015. Making Sense of Miscarriage Online. *Journal of Social Philosophy* 46(1): 106–125.

Harman, E. 2016. Eating Meat as a Morally Permissible Mistake. In *Philosophy Comes to Dinner*, edited by .Chignell, T. Cuneo, & M. Halteman, 215–231. Routledge.

Harré, R. 1990. Embarrassment: A Conceptual Analysis. In *Shyness and Embarrassment: Perspectives from Social Psychology*, edited by R Crozier, 181–204. Cambridge University Press.

Haybron, D. 2008. *The Pursuit of Unhappiness*. Oxford University Press.

Heasman, B., & Gillespie, A. 2019. Learning How to Read Autistic Behavior from Interactions between Autistic People. *Behavioral and Brain Sciences* 42: 25–26. https://doi.org/10.1017/S0140525X18002364.

Heavey, L., Philips, W., Baron-Cohen, S., & Rutter, M. 2000. The Awkward Moments Test: A Naturalistic Measure of Social Understanding in Autism. *Journal of Autism and Developmental Disorders* 30(3): 225–236.

Hebl, M. R., Tickle, J., & Heatherton, T. F. 2000. Awkward Moments in Interactions between Nonstigmatized and Stigmatized Individuals. In *The Social Psychology of stigma*, edited by T. F. Heatherton, R. E. Kleck, M. R. Hebl, & J. G. Hull, 275–306. Guilford Press.

Hendrickson, J. 2023. Why I Dread Saying My Own Name. *The Atlantic*, January 11. https://www.theatlantic.com/ideas/archive/2023/01/stuttering-life-on-delay-book-speech-therapy/672691

Hochschild, A. 1979. Emotion Work, Feeling Rules, and Social Structure. *American Journal of Sociology* 85(3): 551–575.

Holt-Lunstad, J., Smith, T. B., Layton, J. B. 2010. Social Relationships and Mortality Risk: A Meta-Analytic Review. *PLoS Medicine* 7(7): e1000316. https://doi.org/10.1371/journal.pmed.1000316.

Inglis, D. 2001. *A Sociological History of Excretory Experience: Defecatory Manners and Toiletry Technologies*. Edwin Mellen Press.

Jaggar, A. 1989. Love and Knowledge: Emotion in Feminist Epistemology. *Inquiry*. 32(2): 151–176.

Joyce, R. 2006. *The Evolution of Morality*. MIT Press.

Kardas, M., Kumar, A., & Epley, N. 2022. Overly Shallow?: Miscalibrated Expectations Create a Barrier to Deeper Conversation. *Journal of Personality and Social Psychology* 122(3): 367–398.

Kass, L. R. 1997. The Wisdom of Repugnance: Why We Should Ban the Cloning of Humans. *New Republic* 216: 17–26.

Kawall, J. 2010. The Epistemic Demands of Environmental Virtue. *Journal of Agricultural and Environmental Ethics* 23(1–2): 109–128.

Kekes, J. 1992. Disgust and Moral Taboos. *Philosophy* 67(262): 431–446.

Kelly, D. 2013. *Yuck! The Nature and Significance of Disgust*. MIT Press.

Kelly, D. 2020. Internalized Norms and Intrinsic Motivation: Are Normative Motivations Psychologically Primitive? *Emotion Review*, June: 36–45.

Kelly, D. 2021. Charlie Kurth, The Anxious Mind: An Investigation into the Varieties and Virtues of Anxiety. *Ethics* 132(1): 249–255.

Kelly, D., & Davis, T. 2018. Social Norms and Human Normative Psychology. *Social Philosophy and Policy* 35(1): 54–76.

Kelly, D., & Setman, S. 2021. The Psychology of Normative Cognition. In *The Stanford Encyclopedia of Philosophy*, edited by Edward N. Zalta. https://plato.stanford.edu/archives/spr2021/entries/psychology-normative-cognition/. Accessed 3/17/22.

Kelly, T. 2008. Disagreement, Dogmatism, and Belief Polarization. *Journal of Philosophy* 105(10): 611–633.

Keltner, D., & Buswell, B. N. 1997. Embarrassment: Its Distinct Form and Appeasement Functions. *Psychological Bulletin* 122(3): 250–270.

Kidd, I. 2016. Intellectual Humility, Confidence, and Argumentation. *Topoi* 35(2): 395–402.

Kim, M. 2015. Pay Secrecy and the Gender Wage Gap in the United States. *Industrial Relations* 54: 648–667.

King, R. 2021. I Married Jordan Catalano. *Electric Literature* June 17. https://electricliterature.com/i-married-jordan-catalano/

Kleinke, C. L. 1986. Gaze and Eye Contact: A Research Review. *Psychological Bulletin* 100(1): 78.

Klitzman, R. 2020. If You See Someone Not Wearing a Mask, Do You Say Something? *The New York Times*, September 10, updated October 5. https://www.nytimes.com/2020/09/10/well/live/mask-shaming.html

Kotsko, A. 2010. *Awkwardness: An Essay*. O Books.

Koudenburg, N., Postmes, T. & Gordijn, E.H. 2011. Disrupting the Flow: How Brief Silences in Group Conversations Affect Social Needs. *Journal of Experimental Social Psychology* 47(2): 512–515.

Kreuger, J., & Salice, A. 2021. Towards a Wide Approach to Improvisation. In *Improvisation: The Competence(s) of Not Being in Control*, edited by J. McGuirk, S. Ravn, & S. Høffding, 50–69. Routledge.

Kreuz, R., & Roberts, R. 2017. *Getting Through: The Perils and Pleasures of Cross-Cultural Communication*. MIT Press.

Kukla, R. 2014. Performative Force, Convention, and Discursive Injustice. *Hypatia* 29(2): 440–457.

Kurth, C. 2018. *The Anxious Mind*. MIT Press.

Lanciano, T. & Curci, A. 2021. Psychopathic Traits and Self-Conscious Emotions: What Is the Role of Perspective Taking Ability? *Current Psychology* 40(5): 2309–2317.

LeBesco, K. 2010. Fat Panic and the New Morality. In *Against Health: How Health Became the New Morality*, edited by J. Metzl & A. Kirkland, 72–82. New York University Press.

Leddy, K. 2023. When There's No Word Like "Widow." *The New York Times*, February 11. https://www.nytimes.com/2023/02/11/style/grief-loss-sibling.html

Lewis, D. 1969. *Convention*. Harvard University Press.

Levinson, J., ed. 2013. *Suffering Art Gladly: The Paradox of Negative Emotions in Art*. Palgrave MacMillan.

Levinson, S. 2016. Turn-Taking in Human Communication. *Trends in Cognitive Sciences* 20(1): 6–14.

Lickel, B., Schmader, T., & Spanovic, M. 2007. Group-Conscious Emotions: The Implications of Others' Wrongdoings for Identity and Relationships. In *The Self-Conscious Emotions: Theory and Research*, edited by R. Robins, J. Tracy, & J. P. Tangney, 351–370. Guilford.

Life Magazine. 1927. Our Foolish Contemporaries. *Life* 90: 32.

Lord, C. G., Ross, L., and Lepper, M. R. 1979. Biased Assimilation and Attitude Polarization: The Effects of Prior Theories on Subsequently Considered Evidence. *Journal of Personality and Social Psychology* 37(11):2098–2109.

Losse, K. Sex and the Startup: Men, Women, and Work. *Model View Culture*, March 17, 2014. https://modelviewculture.com/pieces/sex-and-the-startup-men-women-and-work. Accessed 10/5/22.

Machery, E. 2012. Delineating the Moral Domain. *Baltic International Yearbook of Cognition, Logic and Communication* 7(1): 1–14. https://doi.org/10.4148/biyclc.v7i0.1777.

Machery, E. 2018. Morality: A Historical Invention. In *Atlas of Moral Psychology*, edited by K. Gray & J.Graham, 259–265. Guilford Press.

Madera, J. M., & Hebl, M. R. 2012. Discrimination against Facially Stigmatized Applicants in Interviews: An Eye-Tracking and Face-to-Face Investigation. *Journal of Applied Psychology* 97(2): 317–330.

Maibom, H. 2010. The Descent of Shame. *Philosophy and Phenomenological Research* 80(3): 566–594.

Maitra, I. 2018. New Words for Old Wrongs. *Episteme* 15(3): 345–362.

Manne, K. 2018. *Down Girl: The Logic of Misogyny*. Oxford University Press.

Manne, K. 2024. *Unshrinking*. Crown.

Margolis, E. 2001. *The Hidden Curriculum in Higher Education*. Routledge.

May, J. 2018. The Limits of Appealing to Moral Disgust. In *The Moral Psychology of Disgust*, edited by N. Strohminger & V. Kumar, 51–170. Rowman & Littlefield.

Medina, J. 2013. *The Epistemology of Resistance*. Oxford University Press.

Medina, J. 2017. Varieties of Hermeneutical Injustice. In *The Routledge Handbook of Epistemic Injustice*, edited by I. James Kidd, G. Pohlhaus, & J. Médina, 41–52. Routledge.

Menninghaus, W., Wagner, V., Hanich, J., Wassiliwizky, E., Jacobsen, T., & Koelsch, S. 2017. The Distancing-Embracing Model of the Enjoyment of Negative Emotions in Art Reception. *Behavioral and Brain Sciences* 40:1–58.

Menza, K. 2018. The Least Awkward Way to Talk About Salary With Your Co-Workers. *Mic.com*, July 18. https://www.mic.com/articles/190373/stories-that-pay-off-why-do-we-get-so-mad-when-others-show-their-financial-privilege

Milgram, S., & Sabini, J. 1978. On Maintaining Urban Norms: A Field Experiment in the Subway. In *Advances in Environmental Psychology*, edited by A. Baum, J. Singer, & S. Valins, 31–40. Erlbaum.

Miller, R. 1996. *Embarrassment: Poise and Peril in Everyday Life*. Guilford Press.

Miller, R. 2014. Embarrassment and Social Anxiety Disorder: Distant Cousins or Fraternal Twins? In *Social Anxiety (Third Edition): Clinical, Developmental, and Social Perspectives*, edited by S. G. Hofmann & P. M. DiBartolo, 117–140. Elsevier.

Miller, R. & Tangney, J. 1994. Differentiating Embarrassment and Shame. *Journal of Social and Clinical Psychology* 13(3): 273–287.

Miller, W. 1993. *Humiliation*. Cornell University Press.
Mirnig, N., Stollnberger, G., Miksch, M., Stadler, S., Giuliani, M., &Tscheligi, M. 2017. To Err Is Robot: How Humans Assess and Act toward an Erroneous Social Robot. *Frontiers in Robotics and AI* 4: 21. https://doi.org/10.3389/frobt.2017.00021.
Moulton, J. 1983. A Paradigm of Philosophy: The Adversary Method. In *Discovering Reality*, edited by S. Harding & M. B. Hintikka. Synthese Library, 161. Springer. https://doi.org/10.1007/0-306-48017-4_9
Munch-Jurisic, D. 2020. The Right to Feel Comfortable: Implicit Bias and the Moral Potential of Discomfort. *Ethical Theory and Moral Practice* 2020(23): 237–250. https://doi.org/10.1007/s10677-020-10064-5.
Munch-Jurisic, D. 2021. Lost for Words: Anxiety, Well-Being, and the Costs of Conceptual Deprivation. *Synthese* 199: 13583–13600.
Murata, K. 1994. Intrusive or Co-Operative? A Cross-Cultural Study of Interruption. *Journal of Pragmatics* 21(4): 385–400.
Ngai, S. 2005. *Ugly Feelings*. Harvard University Press.
Nguyen, C. T. 2020. The Arts of Action. *Philosopher's Imprint* 20(14): 1–27.
Nussbaum, M. 2004. *Hiding from Humanity: Disgust, Shame, and the Law*. Princeton University Press.
Nussbaum, M. 2016. *Anger and Forgiveness: Resentment, Generosity, Justice*. Oxford University Press.
O'Brien, L. 2020. Shameful Self-Consciousness. *European Journal of Philosophy* 28: 545–566.
Olberding, A. 2016. Etiquette: A Confucian Contribution to Moral Philosophy. *Ethics* 126: 422–446.
Olberding, A. 2019. *The Wrong of Rudeness: Learning Modern Civility from Ancient Chinese Philosophy*. Oxford University Press.
Olin, L. 2022. Comic Disagreement. In *Essays in Honor of Allan Gibbard*, edited by D. Plunkett & W. Dunaway, 319–340. Maize Books.
Orth, T. 2022. How Tolerant Are Americans of Awkward Situations? *Today. YouGov.com*. October 19. https://today.yougov.com/topics/society/articles-reports/2022/10/19/how-tolerant-are-americans-awkward-situations.
Packard, C., Boelk, T., Andres, J., Edwards, C., Edwards, A., & Spence, P. R. 2019. The Pratfall Effect and Interpersonal Impressions of a Robot That Forgets and Apologizes. In *2019 14th ACM/IEEE International Conference on Human-Robot Interaction (HRI)*, 524–525. IEEE.
Parrott, W. G. 2004. Appraisal, Emotion Words, and the Social Nature of Self-Conscious Emotions. *Psychological Inquiry* 15(2): 136–138.
Peters, U. 2021. How (Many) Descriptive Claims about Political Polarization Exacerbate Polarization. *Journal of Social and Political Psychology* 9(1): 24–36. https://doi.org/10.5964/jspp.5543.
Plakias, A. 2018. The Response Model of Moral Disgust. *Synthese* 195(12): 5453–5472.

Pohlhaus, G., Jr. 2012. Relational Knowing and Epistemic Injustice: Toward a Theory of "Willful Hermeneutical Ignorance." *Hypatia* 27(4): 715–735.
Pohlhaus, G. 2020. Epistemic Agency under Oppression. *Philosophical Papers* 49(2): 233–251. https://doi.org/10.1080/05568641.2020.1780149.
Pontari, B. A., & Schlenker, B. R. 2000. The Influence of Cognitive Load on Self-Presentation: Can Cognitive Busyness Help as Well as Harm Social Performance? *Journal of Personality and Social Psychology* 78(6): 1092–1108.
Prentice, D. & Miller, D. 1993. Pluralistic Ignorance and Alcohol Use on Campus: Some Consequences of Misperceiving the Social Norm. *Journal of Personality and Social Psychology* 64(2): 243–256.
Prentice, D., & Miller, D. 1996. Pluralistic Ignorance and the Perpetuation of Social Norms by Unwitting Actors. *Advances in Social Psychology* 28:161–206.
Protasi, S. *The Philosophy of Envy*. 2021. Cambridge University Press.
Purshouse, L. 2001. Embarrassment: A Philosophical Analysis. *Philosophy* 76(4): 515–540.
Quora.com, Can Psychopaths Feel Awkwardness? https://www.quora.com/Can-psychopaths-feel-awkwardness. Accessed 1/11/23.
Raymond, L., Weldon, S., Kelly, D., Arriaga, X., & Clark, A. 2014. Making Change: Norm-Based Strategies for Institutional Change to Address Intractable Problems. *Political Research Quarterly* 67(1): 197–221.
Rhodes, S. 2016. *This Is Awkward*. Nelson Books.
Riggle, N. 2016. High Five! Awesomeness as the Imperative of Our Time. *Aeon Magazine*, February 9, 2016.
Riggle, N. 2017. *On Being Awesome: A Unified Theory of How Not to Suck*. Penguin.
Rini, R. 2021. *The Ethics of Microaggression*. Routledge.
Roberts, S. 2020. Sophia Farrar Dies at 92; Belied Indifference to Kitty Genovese Attack. *The New York Times*, September 2. https://www.nytimes.com/2020/09/02/nyregion/sophia-farrar-dead.html
Ronson, J. 2015. *So You've Been Publicly Shamed*. Riverhead Books.
Rozin, P. 1997. Moralization. In *Morality and Health*, edited by A. Brandt & P. Rozin, 379–401. Routledge.
Ruzich, E., Allison, C., Smith, P., Watson, P., Auyeung, B., Ring, H., & Baron-Cohen, S. 2016. Subgrouping Siblings of People with Autism: Identifying the Broader Autism Phenotype. *Autism Research* 9(6): 658–665.
Sabini, J., Siepmann, M., Stein, J., & Meyerowitz, M. 2000. Who Is Embarrassed by What? *Cognition and Emotion* 14(2): 213–240. https://doi.org/10.1080/026999300378941.
Sabini, J., Siepmann, M., & Stein, J. 2001. The Really Fundamental Attribution Error in Social Psychological Research. *Psychological Inquiry* 12(1): 1–15. https://doi.org/10.1207/S15327965PLI1201_03.
Sabini, J., & Silver, M. 1982. *Moralities of Everyday Life*. Oxford University Press.

Sabini, J., & Silver, M. 1997. In Defense of Shame: Shame in the Context of Guilt and Embarrassment. *Journal for the Theory of Social Behaviour* 27: 1–15.

Sale, A. 2021. *Let's Talk about Hard Things*. Simon & Schuster.

Sanderson, C. 2020. *The Bystander Effect: The Psychology of Courage and Inaction*. William Morrow.

Saul, J. 2013. Implicit Bias, Stereotype Threat, and Women in Philosophy. In *Women in Philosophy: What Needs to Change?*, edited by K. Hutchison & F. Jenkins, 39–60. Oxford University Press.

Schank, R. C., & Abelson, R. P. 1977. *Scripts, Plans, Goals and Understanding: An Inquiry into Human Knowledge Structures*. Lawrence Erlbaum.

Scully, J. 2010. Hidden Labor: Disabled/Nondisabled Encounters, Agency and Autonomy. *International Journal of Feminist Approaches to Bioethics* 3(2): 25–42.

Semper, J. V. O., & Blasco, M. 2018. Revealing the Hidden Curriculum in Higher Education. *Studies in Philosophy and Education* 37(5): 481–498.

Shepperd, J., & Arkin, R. 1990. Shyness and Self-Presentation. In *Shyness and Embarrassment: Perspectives from Social Psychology*, edited by R. Crozier, 286–314. Cambridge University Press.

Silver, M., Sabini, J., & Parrott, W. G. 1987. Embarrassment: A Dramaturgic Account. *Journal for the Theory of Social Behaviour* 17(1): 47–61.

Slingerland, E. 2015. *Trying Not To Try*. Crown.

Smuts, A. 2009. Art and Negative Affect. *Philosophy Compass* 4(1): 39–55.

Stalnaker, R. 1978. Assertion. In *Syntax and Semantics*, edited by P. Cole, 315–332. Academic Pres.

Stohr, K. 2012. *On Manners*. Routledge/Taylor & Francis.

Stohr, K. 2018. The Etiquette of Eating. In *The Oxford Handbook of Food Ethics*, edited by T. Doggett, 700–721. Oxford University Press.

Strohl, M. 2012. Horror and Aesthetic Ambivalence. *Journal of Aesthetics and Art Criticism* 70(2): 203–212.

Tangney, J. 1995. Shame and Guilt in Interpersonal Relationships. In *Self-Conscious Emotions*, J. Tangney & K. Fisher, 114–139. Guilford Press.

Tangney, J. P., Miller, R. S., Flicker, L., & Barlow, D. H. 1996. Are Shame, Guilt, and Embarrassment Distinct Emotions? *Journal of Personality and Social Psychology* 70(6): 1256–1269.

Tannen, D. 1981. The Machine Gun Question: An Example of Conversational Style. *Journal of Pragmatics* 5(5): 383–397.

Tashiro, T. 2017. *Awkward: The Science of Why We're Socially Awkward and Why That's Awesome*. William Morrow.

Tavris, C. 1974. The Frozen World of the Familiar Stranger. *Psychology Today* 8: 71–80.

Taylor, G. 1985. *Pride, Shame, and Guilt: Emotions of Self-Assessment*. Oxford University Press.

Terzi, L. 2004. The Social Model of Disability: A Philosophical Critique. *Journal of Applied Philosophy* 21(2): 141–157.

Thomas, K., DeScioli, P., & Pinker, S. 2018. Common Knowledge, Coordination, and the Logic of Self-Conscious Emotions. *Evolution and Human Behavior* 39: 179–190.

Thomas, K. A., DeScioli, P., Haque, O. S., & Pinker, S. 2014. The Psychology of Coordination and Common Knowledge. *Journal of Personality and Social Psychology* 107(4): 657–676.

Thomason, K. 2015. Shame, Violence, and Morality. *Philosophy and Phenomenological Research* 91(1):1–24.

Tiffany, K. 2022. How Did We Get So Cringe? *The Atlantic*, January 15. https://www.theatlantic.com/technology/archive/2022/01/cringe-culture-everywhere/621272/

Timpe, K. 2022. Cognitive Disabilities, Forms of Exclusion, and the Ethics of Social Interactions. *Journal of Philosophy of Disability* 2: 157–184.

Tosi, J., & Warmke, B. 2020. *Grandstanding: The Use and Abuses of Moral Talk.* Oxford University Press.

Tracy, J., Robins, R., & Tangney, J., eds. 2007. *The Self-Conscious Emotions: Theory and Research.* Guilford Press.

Tsoulis-Reay, A. 2017. 5 Men on Why They Didn't Stop Harassment at Work. *The Cut*, November 17. https://www.thecut.com/2017/11/men-on-why-they-didnt-stop-sexual-harassment-at-work.html

Tuana, N. 2004. Coming to Understand: Orgasm and the Epistemology of Ignorance. *Hypatia* 19(1): 194–232.

Van Norden, B. 2011. *Introduction to Classical Chinese Philosophy.* Hackett.

Visser, M. 1991. *The Rituals of Dinner.* Grove Weidenfeld.

Waldron, J. 1981. A Right to Do Wrong. *Ethics* 92(1): 21–39.

Weaver, J., Fisher, R., & Ehney, K., 2002. In Search of the "Pratfall Effect": How General and Reliable Is This Phenomenon? *Representative Research in Social Psychology* 26: 34–43.

Whitcomb, D., Battaly, H., Baehr, J., & Howard-Snyder, D. 2017. Intellectual Humility: Owning Our Limitations. *Philosophy and Phenomenological Research* 94(3): 509–539.

White, D., Hillier, A., Frye, A., & Makrez, E. 2019. College Students' Knowledge and Attitudes Towards Students on the Autism Spectrum. *Journal of Autism and Developmental Disorders* 49(7): 2699–2705.

Wildman, S. 2017. I Was Harrassed at The New Republic. I Spoke Up. Nothing Happened. *Vox*, November 9. https://www.vox.com/first-person/2017/11/9/16624588/new-republic-harassment

Wu, K. 2022. It's Gotten Awkward to Wear a Mask. *The Atlantic*, October 19. https://www.theatlantic.com/health/archive/2022/10/americans-no-longer-wear-masks-covid/671797/

Wylie, A. 2012. Feminist Philosophy of Science: Standpoint Matters. *Proceedings and Addresses of the American Philosophy Association* 86(2): 47–76.

Yancy, G. 2008. Elevators, Social Spaces, and Racism. *Philosophy and Social Criticism* 34(8): 843–876.

Zheng, R. 2021. Moral Criticism and Structural Injustice. *Mind* 130(518): 503–535. https://doi.org/10.1093/mind/fzaa098.

Zoccola, P., Green, M., Karoutsos, E., Katona, S., & Sabini, J. 2011. The Embarrassed Bystander: Embarrassability and the Inhibition of Helping. *Personality and Individual Differences* 51: 925–929.

Index

For the benefit of digital users, indexed terms that span two pages (e.g., 52–53) may, on occasion, appear on only one of those pages.

activism, 140–42
Ahmed, Sarah 62, 139–40
ambiguity
    awkwardness and, 5, 10, 11, 20, 28
    in awkward situations, 29–30, 31, 33
    bystander effect and, 105–7
    emotions and feelings, 59, 60–61
    moral awkwardness and, 92–93, 105–11, 112, 113–14, 117–18
    normative status of awkwardness and, 148–49, 158, 162–63, 168
    silence and, 113–14, 119–20, 125, 140–41, 147
    in social situations, 75–76, 77, 78–81, 83
anxiety, 35, 41–42, 58–61, 91
attunement, 3, 61–63, 125, 140, 146
autism, 34n.17, 35–36, 39–40, 131–33, 137–38
autonomy, 95, 96
awkward moments test, 39–40
awkwardness. *See also* conversational awkwardness; feelings/feeling awkward; moral awkwardness; normative status of awkwardness; self-consciousness awkwardness; social situation awkwardness
    analysis of, 22–30
    characterization of, 5, 67
    cringing in response to, 42–46
    defined, 7–8
    deviance and, 19–21
    etiquette and, 12–14
    etymology of, 8–10
    everything as, 31–32
    feelings of, 23–25
    in interactions, 25–28, 32, 49, 65–66, 78, 150, 158–59, 160
    online, 164–66
    physically awkward, 9n.2, 62–63
    power and, 136–40
    privilege and, 136–40
    psychology of, 2n.1, 4–5, 34
    radical, 27
    social change and, 1
    sources in everyday life, 10–12
    unscripted socializing, 15–18
    weaponization of, 127–30
awkward silence. *See also* silence
    activism and, 140–42
    discursive disadvantage, 130–36
    epistemic injustice, 92, 118, 120–21, 122, 123–27, 131
    hermeneutical gap, 122, 123–27, 129
    ignorance, as social construct, 120–23
    overview of, 119–20
    shame and, 142–46
    social scripts and, 123–27, 136–40
    taboos and, 142–46

awkward silence (*cont.*)
  weaponization of awkwardness, 127–30
awkward situations. *See also* social situation awkwardness
  emotions and feelings, 38–39, 45–46, 59, 61–62
  normative status of awkwardness and, 159–61, 163, 165
  overview of, 3–4, 17–18, 22, 24, 29n.13, 30, 33–36
  silence and, 134–35, 139, 143–44
  in social situations, 65–67, 68, 75–76, 79, 84–85

Berlant, Lauren, 66–67
blame/blameworthiness, 11, 33, 94–95, 101–3, 151–54, 156
Brownlee, Kimberley, 115–16
bystander effect, 104–7

Calhoun, Cheshire, 101–2, 145
Carroll, Noël, 67, 67n.4
characterization of awkwardness, 5, 67
comedy, awkward 65–68
conceptual engineering, 154–58
Confucian ethics, 69
conscious expectations, 16
consciousness-raising, 124, 164–65
conversational awkwardness
  moral awkwardness and, 102, 108–9, 111–12, 114, 117–18
  normative status of awkwardness and, 148, 154–55, 160–61, 164–65
  overview of, 3, 7, 19–20, 22–23, 30
  silence and, 119–20, 124, 128–29, 134–35, 147
  social cues and, 34
  social scripts and, 16, 25–27
  in social situations, 73, 80
  timing patterns, 16–18
  unintended cross-talk, 16, 17–18

COVID-19 pandemic, 76–77, 93
cringe comedy, 65–68, 158–59
cringing, 42–46

deviance, 19–21
discomfort
  awkwardness and, 2–3, 6, 19–20, 23–24, 28–29, 30, 33, 35
  emotions and feelings, 38–39, 41, 45–46, 58–59, 61, 62–63
  moral awkwardness and, 97–98, 114–15, 116–17
  normative status of awkwardness and, 153, 164–65
  silence and, 124–25, 129, 133–36, 145–46
  in social situations, 84
  uncomfortableness, 1, 19–20, 23–25, 28–29, 31–33, 48–49, 55, 58–61, 93, 97–98, 121, 128, 133–35
discredit, 52–53, 134n.11
disgust, 13–14, 32, 34n.16, 43
dispositional analysis, 34–35
disruptions, 20–21, 62–63, 66–67, 68, 75–76, 140

elevator effect, 87–88
embarrassment
  awkwardness *vs.*, 19–20, 26–27
  bystander effect and, 105–7
  feeling awkward and, 48–56
  immunity from, 39–42
  normative status of awkwardness and, 167–68
  shame and, 38, 51–52, 56–58
  sticky situations and, 50–51, 53–55
emotions. *See also* feelings/feeling awkward
  ambiguity and, 59, 60–61
  anxiousness, 35, 41–42, 58–61, 91
  awkward silence and, 130–36

in awkward situations, 38–39, 45–46, 59, 61–62
discomfort and, 38–39, 41, 45–46, 58–59, 61, 62–63
expressions of, 130–36
negative emotions, 2, 65–66
self-conscious emotions, 46–48
social anxiety, 35, 60
uncertainty and, 38–39, 52, 55, 58–60
empathy, 39–41, 66–67, 133, 140
epistemic injustice, 92, 118, 120–21, 122, 123–27, 131
etiquette, 12–14
everyday awkwardness, 10–12
eye contact, 13–14, 18, 33, 34–35, 43, 160

false shame, 144–45
Farrar, Sophia, 104
faux pas, 50–52, 53–54
feelings. *See also* emotions; shame
in awkward situations, 38–39, 45–46, 59, 61–62
embarrassment and, 48–56
immunity from, 39–42
misattunement, 61–63
overview of, 23–25, 38–39
shame and, 56–58
uncomfortableness, 58–61
varied experiences of, 42–46
formative moral criticism, 102–4
Fricker, Miranda, 120–23
friendship
awkwardness and, 7, 12, 19–20, 25–26, 28
awkward silence and, 129, 136–37, 147
moral awkwardness and, 94–96, 98–100, 103, 117–18
normative status of awkwardness and, 154–55
social awkwardness and, 73, 78, 87

Genovese, Kitty, 104
Goffman, Erving, 13, 22, 26–27, 87–88
gossip, 29n.13, 46–47
guilt, 3, 20–21, 39, 47–48, 97

Harbin, Ami, 112–13, 124
Haybron, Dan, 61–62
hermeneutical gap, 122, 123–27, 129
hermeneutical injustice, 122, 131, 136–37
hesitation, 7, 28–30, 43, 71–72, 76, 97–98, 106, 125
horror, 66–67
humiliation, 2, 40–41, 49, 56
humor, 158–59. *See also* comedy, awkward

identity, 83–89
ignorance, 120–23
improvisation, 158–64
inclusivity, 115–16, 138, 144, 150–51, 153–54, 157, 159–60, 166
intercorporeal experience, 62

James, William, 121

Kostko, Adam 2n.1, 10–11, 40, 41, 42, 67–68
Kukla, Quill 127–30

loneliness, 11, 23, 57, 60, 93, 107–8, 115, 117–18, 132–33, 166

Manne, Kate, 83–84, 126, 133–34
manners, 13–14, 69–72, 87
Milgram, Stanley, 91–93, 116, 117–18
Miller, Rowland, 11, 19–20, 49, 55
Miller, William, 2, 56, 105
misattunement, 61–63
moral awkwardness
ambiguity and, 92–93, 105–11, 112, 113–14, 117–18

moral awkwardness (*cont.*)
   autonomy and, 95, 96
   bystander effect, 104–7
   discomfort and, 97–98, 114–15, 116–17
moral critique, 3, 93–104, 107, 108–10, 113, 156
moral drift, 113
moral ignorance, 101–2
moral resolve, 111–13
morally awkward problems, 107–13
Munch-Jurisic, Ditte Marie, 59, 61, 124, 152
My So-Called Life 26

negative emotions, 2, 65–66
Ngai, Sianne, 42–43, 66–67
normative status of awkwardness.
   See also social norms
   ambiguity and, 148–49, 158, 162–63, 168
   awkward situations and, 159–61, 163, 165
   conceptual engineering and, 154–58
   conversational awkwardness and, 148, 154–55, 160–61, 164–65
   discomfort and, 153, 164–65
   embarrassment and, 167–68
   humor and, 158–64
   overview of, 148–49
   social scripts and, 154–58, 166–67
   uncertainty and, 148–49, 158–60, 167

physically awkward, 9n.2, 62–63
pluralistic ignorance, 80–83, 106, 113
politeness, 19–20, 97, 114
power 136–40
privilege, 136–40
pronouns, 157–58
proxemics, 18, 165

racism, 140–42
radical awkwardness, 27

reflection, 111–13
resolvism, moral 111–13
Riggle, Nick 161n.91, 163

scripts. *See* social scripts
Seinfeld, 40–41
self-consciousness
   feelings and emotions (*see* self-conscious emotions)
   normative status of awkwardness and, 158–59
   overview of, 1, 2, 5, 20–21, 23–25, 35
   social awkwardness and, 71
self-conscious emotions (SCEs), 21, 38–39, 41–42, 45–48, 57, 58–61
self-presentation, 12, 26
sexual harassment, 6, 7, 85, 94, 120, 122–25, 129, 136, 143
shame
   awkward silence and, 142–46
   embarrassment and, 38, 51–52, 56–58
   false shame, 144–45
   feeling awkward and, 56–58
   self-consciousness and, 20–21
shaming, 99
silence. *See also* awkward silence
   ambiguity and, 113–14, 119–20, 125, 140–41, 147
   awkward situations and, 134–35, 139, 143–44
   discomfort and, 124–25, 129, 133–36, 145–46
   uncertainty and, 130, 142
situationism, 92, 105
social anxiety, 35, 60
social change, 1, 154–55
social conformity, 3
social coordination, 12, 15–16
social cues, 15, 23–24, 34–35, 36, 39, 42, 132
social destabilization, 11

social dysfunction, 2–3, 11
social exclusion, 86, 116–17, 132–33, 144
social expectations, 3, 47–48, 74, 135
social faux pas, 50–51, 53–54
social improvisation, 158–64
social interactions, 1, 6, 8–10, 12, 15, 20–21, 29–32, 38–39, 70–71, 77–78, 115, 117–18, 134–35, 160–61
social isolation, 115, 116–17, 163–64
socially awkward, 34–36, 34n.17, 49, 62, 70–71, 79–80, 94
social motives, 114–17
social nature, 1, 41–42, 61
social norms. *See also* normative status of awkwardness
  overview of, 2, 5, 11, 20–21, 27, 33–34, 35–36
  in social situations, 64, 68–83, 85, 89–90
social scripts. *See also* unscriptedness
  awkward interactions and, 25–28
  awkward silence and, 123–27, 136–40
  normative status of awkwardness and, 154–58, 166–67
  in social situations, 72–84, 86, 88
social situations, awkward. *See also* awkward situations
  aesthetics of awkwardness, 64, 68–72
  ambiguity in, 75–76, 77, 78–81, 83, 85
  discomfort in, 84
  exclusion and, 83–89
  identity and, 83–89
  overview of, 65–67, 68, 75–76, 79, 84–85
  pluralistic ignorance, 80–83
  social norms in, 64, 68–83, 85, 89–90
  uncertainty in, 64, 69–70, 71–72, 76–77, 78
social skills, 11, 70–71, 79, 134–35
somatic confidence, 61–62
sticky situations, embarrassment and 50–51, 53–55
summative moral criticism, 102–4

taboos and awkward silence, 142–46
Taylor, Gabrielle, 52–53
Thatcher, Margaret 17

uncertainty
  as awkward, 1, 3–4, 10, 22, 23–25, 29, 31
  emotions and feelings, 38–39, 52, 55, 58–60
  moral awkwardness and, 92, 97–98, 99–100, 106, 108–11, 112–13, 117–18
  normative status of awkwardness and, 148–49, 158–60, 167
  silence and, 130, 142
  in social situations, 64, 69–70, 71–72, 76–77, 78
uptake, 114, 127–30, 137–38, 141
unscriptedness, 15–18, 19–21, 24–28, 38–39, 55, 109–10, 164–65. *See also* social scripts

violations, 11, 19, 20–21, 46–48, 53–54, 55, 72–73, 75–76, 142
virtue signaling, 99–100

weaponization of awkwardness, 127–30

Zheng, Robin, 102–4, 156